Samuel Colville

The Whigs Supplication

Samuel Colville

The Whigs Supplication

ISBN/EAN: 9783744711265

Printed in Europe, USA, Canada, Australia, Japan

Cover: Foto ©ninafisch / pixelio.de

More available books at **www.hansebooks.com**

Then he a Multitude espies
Approaching him with Shouts and Cries,
He leaves his Victuals, falls a gazing,
Just like a Tupp when he's a grazing.

Morison's Edition of the **Scots Hudibras** *by* S. COLVILLE.

Perth: Printed for R. Morison & Son, Jan.y 2, 1797.

"That roving London flees his view,
He stops to bids it thus adieu."

THE WHIGS SUPPLICATION;

OR, THE SCOTS HUDIBRAS.

A MOCK POEM.

IN TWO PARTS.

BY SAMUEL COLVIL.

ENRICHED WITH A COLLECTION OF SUPERB ENGRAVINGS.

ST. ANDREWS:

PRINTED BY AND FOR JAMES MORISON,
PRINTER TO THE UNIVERSITY.

1796.

THE
AUTHOR'S APOLOGY
TO THE
READER.

CHRISTIAN READER!

VERSES are like ladies faces, good or bad as they are fancied, faith Don Quixote; and Mock Poems which bite not, are like eggs eaten without falt, faith another of the fame metal; that is, whofe tongue was a great deal wifer than his head.

IN thefe following lines I am more tart to none than myfelf: and therefore I may be excufed, if I tell in rhyme how fome ufed me in profe: I fpeak truth, which is expedient to be known, and therefore no lawyer will aver I tranfgrefs the law.

WITH all the world befide, I am like a blind man dealing blows, not knowing whom I hit: If any fhall challenge me that I touch them, I will anfwer, that I knew not so much before they informed me; as answered that famous satirist to a noble Roman, who expostulated with him for smiting him in a poem.

I am many ways wronged: and first, by transcribers, who, stealing copies of my lines, have transmitted them every where, like pictures on the wrong side of arras hangings, spoiled with thrumbs and threads; or like faces disfigured by the pox, great or small, as ye please: or like sermons repeated by children and serving lasses in a Presbyterian family-exercise; or like one of Bishop Andrews' Sermons, repreached the other day by an expectant in his Episcopal trial for the ministry.

I am, secondly, wronged by false copies; and that by men either malicious, to bring me to trouble, or ignorant, not apprehending my scope, who, instead of mending my lines, have marred them all; and who striving to pull me out of the mire, have thrown me into the well, not to wash me, but to drown me; or into the fire, not to dry me, but to burn me.

Thirdly, I am most of all prejudged by the late Dutch war, which occasioned the bringing in of such superfluity of brandy, which, entering the brain of some of the worshippers of Bacchus, hath there hatched glosses of my lines, like that of Orleans, destroying the text.

TO THE READER.

THOSE brandy interpreters may be compared to children espying shapes and figures in the fire; or to those who are giddy with drink, imagining apparitions in the clouds; or to old wives commenting on Merlin's or Rymer's prophecies; or to bad divines expounding the Revelation, who obtrude groundless fancies upon the ignorant multitude for evangelical truths.

IF those gentlemen hit my meaning, any censure is too little for me: if not, no punishment is too great for them; and that for two reasons:

FIRST, because they apply passages of my lines to men of honour, of whom (God is my witness) I did not dream. Secondly, because they made the world believe I am biting those whose wounds I am licking, given by the biting of other dogs.

THESE things considered, it is easy to answer all which is objected against me. And first, some of the Society of Gotham College had an intention to burn my lines, because I bring in Whigs speaking too boldly in the Supplication, and elsewhere. But I answer, if those gentlemen speak as they think, I commend their zeal, but not their wisdom; and whoever shall take the pains to burn them for witches, will lose both coals and labour. I demand of them, if one should pen a play of the powder-plot, and bring in the conspirators, exhorting each other to blow up the parliament-house, who will tax the author of treason? or who will tax the Psalmist of atheism, for averring, 'The fool hath 'said in his heart there is not a God!' All not mere ignorants, know it is permitted to poets, good or bad, to personate a discourse, that is, to bring in rebels speaking treason, and atheists blasphemy; and why may not I, a poetaster, or poet's ape, bring in fools speaking foolishly, and wise men wisely, and yet be neither a wise man nor a fool myself? And if I be neither, I must either be a mixed man, or else nothing. And in effect some call me a mixed man, others nothing: But since those who call me nothing are highly offended at me, they must of necessity confess they are offended at nothing: I am more charitable to them, I think they are something. What sort of thing it is all the world knoweth, whatever it be, it is worse than nothing.

They object, secondly, that, without authority, I have imposed a grievous taxation upon the lieges, in exacting five dollars for every copy, which may be called treason.

But I answer, since I charge them not with horning to make payment, the worst they can call it is but begging; which it is not, but a nameless contract, *Do, ut des*. And, at first, I did not dream of taking money for those lines, until some known bitter enemies to the Presbyterians enforced each of them five dollars on me for a copy: they told me I might as well take money for rhyme, as ministers and lawyers for prose, and physicians for nothing, and worse than nothing. Some pleading, preaching, and curing, it is true, deserves money a great deal better than my lines: but it is as true, that some of all three deserves it worse. If my lines do no good, they do no hurt to the souls, bodies, or estates of any.

SECONDLY, I demand money of no man; yea, I refuse it when it is offered not in jest, until they make it appear they offer it in earnest, which they do many ways. Some throw money on the ground; some on the table; some tell they will have none of my lines, except I take their money; some say I undervalue them when I refuse their money; some say they are abler to give me money than I am to want it; some bid devil break their neck if I take not their money; some bid God damn them if I take not their money; yea I can instruct, that a Sea Captain offered to strike off my head with a shable if I refused his money: but the more moderate put money unawares in the pocket of my coat, which many think I keep unbuttoned on purpose. Mistake me not, Reader; I am not instructing how money should be offered, but how it should not be offered, lest I take it.

THIRDLY, that I am not avaricious appears by my vowing to take no money from ministers and ladies; but they say I take gold. But I answer, they eluded my vow by equivocation, putting gold unawares in the neck of my doublet, and then run away, and I following to restore it, stumbled. They instance I stumbled on purpose that I might not reach them: But they are still mistaken; for a lady having used me so, I followed her to her chamber, and when I endeavoured to return her gold to her pocket, her maid mistaking my meaning, thinking perhaps I was searching for the wrong pocket, taxed me of incivility; so I was necessitated either to keep her gold, or else be thought uncivil to a lady: let any indifferent man judge which was the least of two evils. However, Reader, tempt me not with gold, except thou be in earnest. It dazzleth the eyes of the wise, and therefore no marvel it blind those of a fool.

THE third objection against me, is, that some affirm I am a bad poet. But I answer, that nothing can more offend a poet and a fiddler, than telling them they want skill, if in effect they be unskilful as I am: And, therefore, no marvel if I reply in a fury, that it is most true that I am a bad poet; and yet they are notorious liars in averring it, because they do so out of malice, not knowing whether they speak true or false. All the world knoweth they never made a greater progress in poesy than the making of an ale-house roundelay, and that a bad one. It were base in me to upbraid them with want of skill in their own professions, in which they brag they have such insight: As to one of them, a physician, that he took the piss of a ston'd horse for that of a woman with child: to another, a mineralist, who laid a wager of ten dollars, a piece of brimstone was a piece of silver: to a third, a palmister, to whom when a boy in girl's apparel was brought in to him to have his hand viewed, superciliously pronounced, the girl would have three husbands, bring forth nine children, and die of the tenth. It were most base in me to tell them they are fit for nothing, except some will take them on to be tasters of drink; neither are they fit for that but in the morning; for in the afternoon many times they are in the category of plants, that is, without sense and reason, having the use of no soul but the vegetative. I could instance other things of that nature, but I forbear left the persons be discovered.

SECONDLY, to be a bad poet may well be a shame, it is no sin; neither is it a shame for me in this first essay; withal my intention is to make men laugh, and not to vex them: but bad lines many times causeth more mirth than good ones. Where one laughs at the poems of Virgil, Homer, Ariosto, Du Bartas, &c. twenty will laugh at the poems of John Cockburn, or

THE AUTHOR'S APOLOGY

Mr. Zachary Boyd. What hypochondriac would not presently be cured at the reading of those lines!

> There was a man called Job,
>   Dwelt in the land of Uz,
> He had a good gift of the gob,
>   The same case happen us.

Or of those:

> Absalom hanged on a tree,
>   Crying God's mercy:
> Then Joab came in, angry was he,
>   And put a spear in his arsie.

Or those of John Cockburn:

> Samuel was sent to France,
> To learn to sing and dance,
>   And play upon a fiddle:
> Now he's a man of great esteem,
> His mother got him in a dream,
>   At Culross on a girdle.

For my part, if I were a great man, I would sooner give gold for such lines, than copper for all the heroic oracles of Seneca's Tragedies.

TO THE READER.

IF any have more to object, let them impart it to me: and if I cannot excuse myself in reason, I am willing to satisfy the law. I think it very strange that some grave and reverend men should so wrong their conscience to traduce me, since without hurting their conscience they may speak so much evil of me, and not lie, as I may likewise do of them.

IN the end I give the argument of a second part, which will prove as harmless as a whitred without teeth, except some will be pleased to call cars horns.

ONE word more, Reader, and I shall trouble thee no further: when thou hast perused my lines, and found them a cheat, it cannot but vex thee that thou hast bestowed thy money to no purpose. But I entreat thee to consider, that the only remedy is to conceal the cheat, by commending still my lines to others, that thou may laugh when they shall be cheated as well as thyself: in doing of which thou shalt be a more Christian liar than those who undervalue my lines, albeit they understand them no more than they do the prophet Ezekiel, as appears by their commentaries on that prophet, ready for the press, if they were once dead.

Farewell,

SAMUEL COLVIL.

THE
WHIGS SUPPLICATION.

A
MOCK POEM.

PART I.

ARGUMENT.

AFTER invoking of the muse,
As many learned poets use:
Next is describ'd the time of year
When Whigs in armour did appear:
The *Good-man*'s person, and his weed,
His armour, lady, squire, and steed,
Dog, and pigeon, and his mind,
All allegories, where ye find
Cloth'd with many a senseless word,
Mysterious things not worth a t———;   10
As said one in a rev'rend coat,
Or else he understood them not.

B

As lately when he Scripture-vext,
He forc'd was to fay off his text :
And then ye have a Supplication
Greatly mifconftru'd of the nation :
At firft they difpute how to mend it ;
And then advife by whom to fend it :
Where Knight and Squire each other thump,
As did De Ruyter and Van Trump.   20
    Whoe'er thou art, Mufe, who doft make
By force of brandy, ale, and fack,
Some who both words and matter want,
Admired of the ignorant :
In whom fagacious nofes fnuff ;
Nought worth but plagiary ftuff,
By which they purchafe praife and money,
(When bees have toil'd, drones eat the honey.)
Infpire me with poetic fury,
That I may likewife favour curry :   30
With all men to augment my pack,
By making lines not worth a plack :
Some of eight fyllabs, fome of ten,
Some borrowed from other men,
As Cleveland, Donne, or Tafs divine ;
Some ill tranflated from Marine ;
Some Oedipus cannot unriddle ;
Some founding like a blind man's fiddle,
Obferving neither tune nor time ;
Some nonfenfe to make up the rhyme.   40

Though I speak true, or false, no matter;
If I traduce, some others flatter.
So sundry men were us'd of late,
As they were on or off the state.
Grant that I may curb all backbiters
Of surplice, high-sleev'd gowns, and mitres,
And church-governing paradoxes,
Of Calvin's followers, and Knoxes;
In mystic allegoric tone,
Scarce understood by any one.   50
Grant me to scold, revile, and prat,
Shame fall me if myself knows what.
When rhyme bursts out from breast enrag'd;
Like t—— from puddings overcharg'd;
Some galling, other some to laughter
Moving, like parrot when its taught her.
Hoping my prayer thou wilt hear,
O muse! Have at the time of year,
When Whigs from lurking holes did sally,
And in the open fields did rally.   60

It was about the time when oysters
Abound so with venereous moistures,
That they are used even and morn
By those that do their neighbour horn,
Which doth their prices so enhance,
At England's court and that of France,
That oyster-wives have money ready,
To make their daughter sometime lady;

As doth appear by one of late,
Whose son-in-law bore sway in state.   70
When snow makes dikes and mountains white,
When folks by physic seldom sh——,
Except there be some pocky reason;
When mutton weareth out of season,
Instead of which at ev'ry meal,
When men eat roasted hens and veal;
And those at Forth eat Garvie fishes,
Then fittest to be serv'd in dishes,
Which to the palate pleasing proves,
Like Adriatic Gulf anchoves.   80
When that the black-bird hoarsely whistles,
When trouts and Abercorn muscles
Are stark nought; when that the swallow
Lies sleeping in her own tallow,
Within some subterranean hole;
When under the Antarctic pole
There is no night, under our other
A man cannot discern his brother,
It is so dark; when summers heats
Scorches the Magellanic Straights,   90
And burneth up the corn and hay
About the *Caput Bonae Spei:*
If that be tedious to remember,
It was in Januar or December,
When I did see the out-law Whigs
Lie scatter'd up and down the riggs.

Some had hoggars, some straw boots,
Some uncover'd legs and coots:
Some had halberds, some had durks,
Some had crooked swords like Turks: 100
Some had slings, some had flails,
Knit with eel and oxen tails:
Some had spears, some had pikes,
Some had spades which delved dikes:
Some had guns with rusty ratches,
Some had firy peats for matches:
Some had bows, but wanted arrows,
Some had pistols without marrows:
Some had the coulter of a plough,
Some scythes had men and horse to hough: 110
And some with a Lochaber axe,
Resolv'd to give *Dalzel* his paiks.
Some had crofs-bows, some were flingers,
Some had only knives and whingers:
But most of all, believe who lifts,
Had nought to fight with but their fists.
They had no colours to display,
They wanted order and array.
Their *officers* and *motion-teachers*,
Were very few beside their preachers.   120
Without horse or artil'ry-pieces,
They thought to imitate the Swisses:
When from Navarre they sally'd out,
Tremovile and brave *Trivulce* to rout.

For martial mufic, ev'ry day
They ufed oft to fing and pray;
Which hearts them more when danger comes,
Than others trumpets and their drums.
With fuch provifion as they had,
They were fo ftout, or elfe fo mad,   130.
As to petition once again;
And if the iffue proved vain,
They were refolv'd, with one accord,
To fight the battles of the Lord.

   Upon their head march'd the *Good-man;*
Like *Scanderbeg* or *Tamerlane.*
Dame Nature ftrain'd her utmoft care,
To mould him for a man of war;
A terrible and dreadful foe,
As doth appear from top to toe.   140
The fhape and fafhion of his head,
Was like a cone or pyramid:
Or for to fpeak in terms more grofs,
It was juft like a fugar loaf:
Or like the head of *Rob* the cripple,
Or like the fpear of Magdalen fteeple:
Or like the bottom of a tap,
Or like a furr'd Mufcovia cap.
They who the fouth-eaft countries haunts,
Affirm fuch heads have Turkifh faints;   150
Which as fome learned writers notes
Are here with us call'd idiots.

Because long hair the wit doth lull,
Nought was between heav'n and his skull:
His ears were long and stood upright,
Which did so well become the knight,
That at some distance he seem'd horn'd,
His one eye was with pearl adorn'd;
His other eye look'd so a-squint,
That it was hard to ward his dint.   160
From thence down to his mouth arose,
A mountain rather than a nose;
Upon which savage beasts did feed,
As worms and felkhorns, which with speed
Would eat it up; but he begins
In time to pick them out with pins.
His lips were thick, his mouth was wide,
His teeth each other did bestride;
His tongue was big, though well he meant,
He was not very eloquent.   170
His beard was long, and red, and thin,
Making a ball-green on his chin;
As trees do some time in a wood,
Where horse and oxen gather food.
His arms were stiff like barrow-trams,
His hands were hued like reisted hams.
At finger-ends he never fails
To have the King of Babel's nails,
Which sooner than a knife by half,
Will cut the throat of sheep or calf.   180

When he not loving to be idle,
Turns cook to any penny-bridle.
They fcrap up works about his leaguer,
A great deal ftronger, and far bigger
Than thofe made by *Don Pedro Saa*,.
When *Spinola* befieg'd Breda.
He had a lump upon his back,
Which fome took for a pedlar's pack:
But other fome did it fuppofe
A bag which kept his meal for brofe. 190
But neither conjecture was good,
It was a lump of flefh and blood.
His womb ftood out an ell before,
As far behind his bum and more:
When overcharg'd it made a found,
Which did like earthquake fhake the ground:
With which, as fentry when he fleeps,
His clothes from mice and rats he keeps;
Which to his pockets fwarm like bees,
Finding the fmell of bread and cheefe, 200
Which fev'ral times the fainting knight
Doth take for cordials in the night.
But when the beafts do hear the thunder,
They're fo amaz'd with fear and wonder,
That to the gate go mice and rats,
As faft as if purfu'd by cats.
Was never man in thofe dominions,
About whofe legs were more opinions.

THE WHIGS SUPPLICATION.

Firſt, there are many who avow,
They are like an inverted V: 210
And other ſome do ſtiffly jangle,
That they and thighs make a quadrangle.
Some think, that thighs joining, they gape,
In circular or oval ſhape.
And other ſome there are who avouch
Them ſemi-circles in a touch:
And other ſome there are who tells,
They're ſemi-circles parallels.
But thoſe who on them better look'd,
Say one was ſtraight, the other crook'd: 220
Not as in touching they did make
That famous angle of contact,
Which *Euclid*'s demonſtration ſhows,
If in their juncture you put ſtraws.
The truth is, they in ev'ry thing
Reſemble do a bow and ſtring:
The one ſtraight to the other bending,
Is like a chord an arch ſubtending:
In which ſcheme if ye draw ſome lines,
Ye may have ſecants, tangents, ſigns,   230
Which ale-pot meaſ'ring much enables,
By help of logarithmic tables:
Which queſtions ſooneſt to decide,
For by ſubſtraction they divide,
And multiplieth by addition,
As now doth Popiſh ſuperſtition,

Which multiplieth ev'ry day,
Having some added to its way.
Their entry to that church is fine,
They re-baptise them all with wine ; 240
Which their apostles think far better
To wash away men's sins, than water.
Now all's describ'd to feet and toes,
Which I could not see for his shoes.
Some say his toes, who saw his feet,
Resembled an alphabet,
Greek, Syriac, or Arabic,
Or breviations stenographic ;
Which they do counterfeit like apes,
With great variety of shapes. 250

 You may believe it as your creed,
Such was his armour and his weed.
He wore a pair of pullion breeches,
A yellow doublet with blue stitches ;
A long black cassock o'er his a—,
As he had been the fool of Mars.
He had on each leg a gramash,
A top of lint for his panash,
Which bravely flourish'd in his crest ;
A folded cloak for back and breast, 260.
A glove of plate, which once was worn
By black *Douglas* at Bannockburn.
For head-piece, a cowl lin'd with iron,
Which did his temples so environ,

THE WHIGS SUPPLICATION.

That it would coſt a world of pains
For any to beat out his brains.
A blunderbuſh hung at his back,
Of terrible report and crack,
As have a lower tier of guns,
Shot from a ſhip of many tuns.   270
A horſe he never doth beſtride,
Without a piſtol at each ſide:
And without other two before,
One at either ſaddle tore.
But now when he hath much ado,
He hath one in each pocket too.
A ſword which woundeth deep and wide,
A target of a ſeven-fold hide:
A very ſtrange enchanted lance,
Whoſe touch makes men from ſaddle dance:
As ſometimes of old did another,   281
Belonging to *Angelique*'s brother,
And after to the Engliſh duke,
As mentions *Arioſto*'s book:
And thus with more arms he doth ride,
Than other twenty had beſide.
Whether he gain the day or tine,
He never miſſeth to kill nine;
As doth appear to all who reckons
Juſtly the number of his weapons.   290
Among ten thouſand all alone,
With ev'ry weapon he kills one.

Some say he used to take lives
With whingers, and Kilmarnock knives:
But he thinks that belongs to butchers,
And others, like *Damaeta*'s coutchers.
For when with any he doth swagger,
He seldom useth knife or dagger,
Except they come in wrestling terms,
Permitted by the laws of arms.   300
The laws of knighthood he doth keep,
Not killing men like calves or sheep.
    I ask'd at sev'ral who he was?
Some said he was *Sir Hudibras*,
Deceived by his bulky paunch:
Some said *Don Quixote de la Manche*;
Which was more like than was the other,
In many things he was his brother.
    First, in his head were many fancies,
Bred by the reading of romances.   310
He thought before the day of doom,
The Covenanters would burn Rome,
And trample down the Man of Sin.
He thought the work he would begin;
And to the glory of his nation,
Accomplish all the *Revelation*;
Prat what they please in Popish schools,
Hammond and *Grotius* were but fools,
Who say it is fulfill'd already;
Most think they prayed to our Lady.   320

SCOTS HUDIBRASS.
I askit at several who he was;
Some said he was Sir Hudibras,
Deceived by his bully Ralpho;
So sac this Don Quixot ac to Mambrino.

They aim'd at reconciliation,
Between the Pope and ev'ry nation.
All other things they could pack up,
If ye take not from them the cup;
And they had reason, for in truth
Some think they had a burning drouth.
   Next, like *Don Quixote*, some suppose
He had a lady *Del To-Bose*,
Who never budged from his side,
Upon a pair of sodds astride: 330
By whose sole industry and care,
He manag'd all the Holy war.
We read in greatest warriors lives,
They oft were ruled by their wives.
The world's conqu'ror, *Alexander*,
Obey'd a lady, his commander;
And *Anthony* that drunkard keen,
Was rul'd by his lascivious queen.
King Arthur for his wife's sake,
Wink'd at *Lancelot Du Lake*;   340
Though to his opprobry and scorn,
He cherish'd one himself to horn.
They say, that now are many others,
Who in that case are *Arthur*'s brothers.
So the imperious *Roxalan*,
Made the Great Turk *John Thomson*'s man.
Another warrior all his life,
Was also ruled by his wife;
               C

Albeit before their death arofe,
Some ftrife between them for her pofe.　　350
　　Thirdly, like *Quixote*, he a fquire
Had *Sancho* call'd, to whet his ire,
When in a fury he did wreftle
With giant, or enchanted caftle:
Or like *Don Quixote* with wind-mills,
Or with *Dalzel* at Pentland hills:
Or when like *Perfeus* he was ready
To fight a monfter for a lady:
Being victorious in the ftrife,
He ftill refus'd the nymph to wife;　　360
And that with fuch a modeft grace,
As Fame's knight did the heir of Thrace:
To which fquire the bounteous knight
Promis'd either Man or Wight,
Guernfey or Jerfey, or fome ifle,
With a lord-governor's ftyle,
When he fhould beat his foes afunder,
And bring the whore of Babel under.
　　Laftly, on *Quixote*'s Rofinant
He rode, who took the *Covenant*.　　370
As many think, none of the nation
Could make him take the *Declaration*.
Some endeavour'd to have the horfe
Proclaimed rebel from the crofs;
Which though they did with open throats,
The horfe eats ftill his hay and oats,

Not dreaming that in any thing
He country did offend, or king.
The wifeſt lawyers of the nation
Advis'd him to make appellation;   380
Becauſe it was againſt all reaſon,
To condemn a beaſt for treaſon;
Which reaſon at a tippling can,
Had ſav'd his maſter, the *Good-man.*
If after his rebellious journey,
He had met with a king's attorney,
Who could by law and reaſon ſhow,
He greater beaſt was of the two:
Or with another, who for riches,
Stood for inceſtuous whores and witches;   390
Or any other whom ye liſt,
So they did well anoint his fiſt.

Beſide his horſe he had a dog,
So us'd to traverſe hill and bog,
That he became of ſcent ſo clever,
As to miſs neither hare nor plover.
He turns himſelf in horſe or hog,
As *Monſieur* did *Agrippa's* dog;
To find by his ſagacious noſe,
The counterplotting of his foes,   400
He treads the back ſcent, brings a glove,
And carries letters to his love:
He is a fierce dog, yet moſt civil,
Kills fiſh, whoſe liver frights the devil.

He barks at *Anabaptist*, *Quaker*,
Papist, and *Declaration-taker*.
But he will gently fawn, and stand
To lick a *Covenanter*'s hand.

   Beside his dog he hath a pigeon,
Most do not know of what religion: 410
She was the same, as many fear,
Which once eat pease in *Mah'met*'s ear;
Which when she did the carl did boast,
That he spoke with the Holy Ghost,
His epilepsy for to cover:
If once employ'd she doth not hover,
But will make the whole world's tour,
And come again within an hour.
Sometimes she his orders carries
To the Azores and Canaries,   420
As quarter-mistress, to ordain
In which the first meridian
Should lodged be, for calculation
Of longitudes in navigation.
Sometimes he sends her an embassage,
Out through the north-east Indian passage,
To tell the great Tartarian Cham,
A piece of a Westphalia ham
Is better meat, when hunger nips,
Than collop of live horses hips: 430
That we who here drink sack and brandy,
Well-tempered with sugar-candy,

A great deal better than he fares,
Who drinks horse blood, or milk of mares.
Sometime to Peru, and to Chily
She goes, to tell our prophet Lilly
Foreseeth neither good nor evil,
Abandon'd by his Arctic devil:
Whom the late great frost did compel
To run and warm himself in hell, 440
That she might bring from thence a spirit,
Of greater foresight and of merit,
For to assist the great *diviner*
The better for to win his dinner.
Sometime to Turk she goes, and Sophy,
To tell their water and their coffee,
And their severe slighting of wine
Makes them so with the colic pine;
Which torment is with them so rife,
It cost *Mah'met* the great his life; 450
For when the colic he did take,
And did refuse a cup of sack,
He worried on a windy bubble,
And freed the world of mickle trouble.
If they'll drink wine, they need not fear
Their prophet, for his thousand year
Are now expir'd; all in vain
They expect his return again.
  Thus of his person, armour, weed,
His lady, squire, and of his steed, 460

Dog, and pigeon; for his mind,
He leaves all mortals far behind.
All things created he doth know,
In heav'n above, and earth below:
He solves the questions ev'ry one,
That *Sheba's Queen* ask'd *Solomon;*
Or any other knotty doubt
That can occur the world throughout.
Neither doth he prat and babble,
Like *Pliny* painting out a fable.   470
At first he makes a clear narration,
And then backs all by demonstration.
He knows whether the Great Mogul
Doth drink out of his father's skull;
Or if he makes a chamber-pot
Of that of king of Calecut.
If it be prov'd by any man,
That he is come of *Tamerlan?*
Or if he keeps tobacco cut,
In tortoise-shell or cocoa-nut?   480
If the balm and frankincense keepers,
By rattling drive away the vipers?
Which with such ardour haunts those trees,
As with us garden flow'rs do bees:
Or if they do those serpents choke,
As easterlings their bees do smoke?
Which made two great wits, as men think,
Spend too much paper, pen, and ink.

THE WHIGS SUPPLICATION. 31

If *ichneumon* and *crocodile*
Do fight in Niger as in Nile? 490
Or if we ought to believe them,
Who say *Melchisedec* was not *Shem?*
Which raised once a fifty strife
Between a preacher and his wife.
If any man yet ever born
Did see *phœnix* or *unicorn?*
If there be a *philos'pher's stone?*
If men who have no leg but *one*,
With broad soles, which by tours
Defends their head from sun and show'rs? 500
If the emperor *Prester John*,
Be the offspring of *Solomon?*
If those who lately conquer'd China,
Be the brother's sons of *Dina?*
Who to those north-east parts were turn'd,
When Assur's king Samaria burn'd.
If *Rome*'s founders wolves did suck?
If *Job* in Edom was a duke?
If *Captain Hynd* was a good fellow?
If *Wallace*' beard was black or yellow? 510
Which raised once a great discord
Between a western laird and lord.
If *roasted* eggs be best, or *sodden?*
If *James* the *Fourth* was kill'd at *Flodden?*
Which made two schoolmen borrow swords,
That they might fight after big words.

If *sword* or *surfeit* more men kill?
Who had the better at *Edge-hill*?
Which made two ladies other jeer,
A round head and a cavalier: 520
Both harped so on the seen ruffle,
That it turn'd to a scratch-eye scuffle:
At last both conclude to agree,
Both of them vowing secrecy.
Where meets the brethren of *Cross Rosie*?
What sums the Spaniard in *Potosie*
Gains yearly by their silver mines?
Since thirty-eight, who *wins* or *tines*?
He knows the price of jewels and rings,
And hidden causes of sundry things. 530
As of the compass variation,
Of Nile and Niger's inundation.
Why Ireland wanteth *toad* and *snake*?
Why some men *white*, and some men *black*?
Why *regulus' eye* makes men leave breath?
Why *spiders* bite them dance to death?
Why men *tarantula* do not fear
But at some seasons of the year?
Why *devils music* do not please?
What sort of thing is *ambergrease*? 540
If iron *magnes*, or it iron
Attract? If sea or land environ
That frozen great magnetic rock,
Under the pole; where what a clock

THE WHIGS SUPPLICATION.

There cannot be made any trial,
The one year's half by Phœbus' dial?
By the sea's motion he doth find
A north-east passage to the Ind:
Another he finds by the north-west,
Where *Davis* freezed to his rest;   550
When icy mountains did occur,
And stopt his course to Mar del Zur:
But he hath found a brave device,
That he may free those seas from ice.
He empties all the water, syne
He fills the place with brandy-wine,
Which hardly will congeal with frost,
If whales turn drunk, and fishing lost;
Yet lose we not by that device,
For whale-oil we get Indian spice.   560
All other ways are but a cheat,
To fetch some money from the state.
Its wonder they have shark'd so much,
Both from the English and the Dutch.
He prov'd, on peril of his soul,
Presbyterian rule by *Paul*.
He thought none but a foolish man
Made Antichrist the son of *Dan;*
He thought by the apostles meaning,
Voice negative, and *sole ordaining*,   570
Was the very mystery
Of Antichrist's iniquity,

Which near his own time did begin
To ufher in the Man of Sin.
He thought if bifhops had not been,
A Pope of Rome had ne'er been feen.
But now he thinketh church-government
A thing of fmall or no concernment;
As ready as any ever born
For bifhops, if he had not fworn.   580
If Dutch and Englifh truth report,
He knows about th' Amboyna fort,
If thofe two Indian fhips were funk,
And burnt by Dutch when they were drunk.
Who firft began the war in Guinea?
Where *Holms* and *Ruyter* play'd at pinie.
If groundlefs jealoufies and fears
Yokes Dutch and Englifh by the ears:
Or if it be the Indian trade
That doth produce effects fo fad.   590
He'll tell in Indian pedlars faces,
We dearly buy their cloves and maces.
The war draws blood and money forth,
More than the Indian trade is worth.
He thinks the war fomented be
By Romifh craft and policy,
Which rends the Dutch and us afunder,
To bring reform'd religion under.
When both are broken and brought low,
Like pitchers by a mutual blow,   600

Then they'll force up the Pope again,
And make both ferve the King of Spain:
Who in the Jefuit's fantafy
The world's temporal lord will be,
And meagre thofe who countermine 'em,
The Pope and he will rule between them:
The world in two monarchies,
He with his fword, he with his keys.
If Dutch and Englifh Popifh were,
They would be Popifh ev'ry where; 610
So conclave fathers do conclude,
But fuch conceits do oft delude.

    He finds perfect demonftrations,
The roots of all compos'd equations.
He finds new ways to poifon cats,
Of mud he ferpents makes, and rats.
He finds the *longitude* of places,
Makes bag-pipes with concording *bafes*.
He finds two means *proportionals*,
Which great wits fometimes enthrals. 620
In virtuofo's conventicles,
Eccentrics, orbs, and epicycles,
He finds to be fantaftic *fictions*,
Forg'd to palliate *contradictions*;
Wherewith the late *ftar-gazers* notions
Have involv'd the planet's motions.
To determine he dare venture,
The fun to be the world's centre,

To hold the candle in the middle
Infix'd, while to *Pythagoras'* fiddle, 630
Still firmament with twinkling eyes,
The earth and planets dancing fees;
He *squares* *circles*, *doubles* *cubes*,
Makes moſt admirable *tubes;*
If he at Dover through them glance,
He ſees what hours it is in France,
As he hath prov'd by frequent trial,
On ſteeple, clock, and ſunny dial:
He reads with them another while
Letters diſtant twenty mile; 640
Dutch or Scots I know not whether,
The one is as like as the other.

 If once he level at the moon,
Either at midnight or at noon,
He diſcovers *rivers, hills,*
Steeples, caſtles, and *wind-mills,*
Villages, and *fenced towns,*
With *fuſees, bulwarks,* and *great guns,*
Cavaliers on horſe-back prancing,
Maids about a may-pole dancing: 650
Men in taverns wine carouſing,
Beggars by the high-way louſing,
Soldiers forging ale-houſe brawlings,
To be let go without their lawings.
Stirs in ſtreets by grooms and pages,
Mountebanks playing on ſtages,

THE WHIGS SUPPLICATION. 37

Wild boars ſtrouting out their briſtles,
Black-birds ſtriving who beſt whiſtles:
Throats of larks trumpeting day,
Falcons beating down their prey: 660
Hare and deer croſſing bogs,
Followed at the heels by dogs:
Aſſes braying, lions roaring,
Owls ſcreeching, eagles ſoaring:
Foxes rouſed from their den,
Monkeys imitating men:
Gardens planting, houſes bigging,
States and princes fleets outrigging:
Antic faſhions of apparels,
States and princes picking quarrels: 670
Wars, rebels, horſe-races
Proclaim'd at ſev'ral market places:
Capers bringing in their prizes,
Commons curſing new exciſes:
Young wives old huſbands horning,
Judges drunk ev'ry morning;
Augmenting law-ſuits and diviſions,
By Spaniſh and by French deciſions:
Courtiers their aims miſſing,
Chaplains widow ladies kiſſing: 680
Men to ſell their lands itching,
To pay th' expences of their kitchen:
Frequent changes, ſtates invading,
Pulpits forcing and perſuading:

D

Great jars for cloves and maces,
For bishops, lordships, and their graces:
Lords in stews missing purses,
While pages make their ladies nurses:
Preachers contradicting fast
This year what they preach'd the last; 690
Making in their conscience room,
For a change the year to come:
Some seeking bishoprics in vain,
Wishing Presbytery again:
Lawyers counsels at such rates,
That they cost men their whole estates:
What money men put in their hands,
To get half back they give their lands:
Physicians cheating young and old,
Making both buy death with gold: 700
Not vers'd in Æsculapius ways,
Indicative and critic days
They make too late, or else too soon,
Not knowing the motion of the moon:
Factions in fam'lies and towns,
Ground manur'd by country clowns;
In meadows, corns, grapes, apples,
Outbraving Lombardy and Naples:
Priests diseased of the ripples,
Hirpling through the streets like cripples: 710
Physicians spoiled by the pox,
Hiding their noses with their cloaks:

THE WHIGS SUPPLICATION.

Courtiers cov'ring canker'd festers,
With curled periwigs and plasters;
With wax noses, golden lips,
With pasteboard mending legs and hips;
Using all the art they can,
That they may seem a pretty man,
And free of blemish, like a priest
With Urim Thummim on his breast: 720
Ladies speaking ranting words,
Attir'd like men with vests and swords;
With periwigs and long locks,
Some tax'd for dancing in their smocks;
Making frivolous excuses;
Men pretending to the muses.
Some selling drink, some selling draff,
Some buffoons turn'd to make men laugh:
Some publicans, some busy meddlers,
Some turn'd horse-coupers, some pedlars: 730
Some challenged for dreadful things,
As stealing silver spoons and rings;
Having us'd many wiles before,
That they might put them to the door.
Sundry philosophic asses,
By dictating, teaching classes,
Not taking an account again,
Making boys spend their time in vain.
Some dissipating little mugs,
Containing universal drugs: 740

Physicians crying out amain,
Where they cure one, they poison ten.
Some getting oyster boats to dreg,
Some making satires for to beg:
Being reduced to those wants
By sev'ral avaricious saints,
Who prov'd on them drinking, whoring,
By sland'ring, forging, and perjuring.
At last, for all their fair pretension,
Their quarrel prov'd to be a pension ; 750
Which having got, then for refuge,
They bribe or cheat a silly judge:
Aye purloining, and forbearing,
To stop the cause from farther hearing.
There was no rem'dy for the evil,
All went headlong to the devil.
That father's saying is most true,
Penitent clerks are very few :
Ere any shame shall them betide,
They'll one sin with another hide. 760

 His tube, in higher planets heaven,
Discovers many more than seven.
Jove has his guard, with thunder thumps,
To beat down *covenants* and *rumps :*
And *Saturn* has his pages too ;
When he meets *Jove* there is ado.
Its good to some, and bad to other,
Its never good to all together ;

For some go up, and some go down,
Some gets, and some will lose a crown.   770
They say such things will now appear,
In less than three-and-thirty year:
Great change of government will be,
As all affirm beyond the sea;
But all their practices and wiles,
At this bout will not reach our isles.
All is confined to the main,
And then it will about again.
We need not break our hearts for sorrow,
What's ours to-day is theirs to-morrow.   780
He sees *Mars* sending grooms in ire,
To set the world below on fire,
Raising such fury in mens breasts,
That generals are made of *priests;*
Which them becomes, as all avow,
As well as saddle doth a sow.
He sees those grooms who *Sun* attends,
Blowing on their burnt finger ends;
Among whom *Mercury* doth stand,
Serving the *Sun* with cap in hand.   790
He hath no dwelling of his own,
But is domestic of the *Sun.*
Phœbus and he hath great compassion,
On arts now wearing out of fashion:
Yet some will flourish they foresaw,
Romances, and the canon law.

He sees with *Venus* pages are,
Who pimps were to the god of war:
When jealous *Vulcan* sick of love,
Would needs himself a cuckold prove,   800
Like sev'ral great ones here below,
Though some conceal what they do know.

His tube once levell'd at the sky,
Sundry, yet hid lights doth espy;
Some lesser ones, and some more gross,
Between the Bears and Southern Cross;
Some on *Pegasus*'s hoof,
And some upon his master's love;
And some upon her mother's chair,
And some on *Berenice*'s hair;   810
And some upon the *serpent*'s sting,
And some upon the *eagle*'s wing;
And some upon the *ram*'s horn,
Some on the beard of *Capricorn*;
And some he sees upon the *Bull*,
And some upon *Orion*'s skull;
And some on *Nessus*' mortal foe,
And some on *Cancer*'s mickle toe:
Some on the sails of *Argo*'s ship,
And some on *Antinous*' hip;
And some he sees upon the *Twins*,   820
And some upon the *fishes* fins;
And some he sees on *Libra*'s scale,
And some upon the *Dragon*'s tail,

Which Little Bear and Pole entangles;
And some he sees on the *triangles*:
Some on the *harp*, some on the *swan*,
Some on the *crown*, some on the *cran*;
Some on the *whale*, some on the *trout*,
And some upon the great *dog*'s snout; 830
And some upon the *virgin*'s knees,
On *Crinita* between her thighs,
Which makes her blush, and turn her look
North-east, upon *Boote*'s dock;
Which the base clown regardeth not,
But spurns her backward with his foot,
And almost lames her on the knee,
Which barb'rous incivility
Is evident to any man,
By the globe of *Vatican*. 840

    And finally, that tract of light
Which we see in a frosty night,
And caused philosophic jars,
He finds to be the light of stars;
Which just so shining he doth mark,
As haddocks heads do in the dark.

    Solve sev'ral questions he can,
Scarce solvable by any man:
If number of stars be odd or even?
What's beyond the utmost heaven? 850
If substance of the heav'ns be mix'd?
If stars do move in orbs infix'd?

Or if they move as others clatter,
As fowl in air, or fish in water?
Since Jewish sabbath is begun,
And ends with setting of the sun,
How that sabbath observ'd can be
Beyond the sixty-eighth degree
Of latitude; since antipodes,
In sunshining, have such odds.   860
How both sabbaths observation
Jumps with the sabbath of creation:
The one and other question
Sorely puzzled Solomon,
In that great dispute that between
Was him and that Arabian queen,
Or Ethiopian, as some other,
Who make her *Prester John*'s mother.

 Against the late star-gazers schism,
And *Argolus*' paralogism,   870
He finds comets are plac'd no where
But in some region of the air.
He finds with admirable speed,
Their parallaxes by a thread.
He finds their eyes perceive not well,
Or else *dioptrics* make them reel;
And that their brain's not worth a t——,
Who call them *Via Lactea*'s curd.
The same he thinks of many others,
Who say they are new stars half-brothers: 880

Of which laſt if he eſpy one,
He bids—let God's ſecrets alone.
He finds both comets and eclipſes,
But pretty fortune-telling gipſies.
The like uncertainty he ſees
In change of *eccentricities*.
But he foreſees by prophets *unction*,
Th' effects of a great *conjunction*.
Before the age begin again,
Spain ſhall have France, or France have Spain;
The monarchy ſhall ſpread no further, 891
If Dutch and Engliſh hold together:
And though they do, great tribulation
Follows a Gothic inundation,
Spreading from Pomer into Scluſe,
In defence of the Flower-de-luce.
Their mutiny for want of pay,
Proves to the French a diſmal day.
Then Engliſh ſhall ſay, God be thanked,
The French are like fleas in a blanket, 900
They ſoon ſkipt out as they did in,
Their conqueſt ends ere it begin:
They mar all by unſtable carriage,
As in their old Italian voyage,
When quite forſaken of their helps,
They firſt brought *ſhankers* o'er the Alps.

 He doth foreſee another wonder,
Nations in place and hearts aſunder,

Shall shortly be conjoin'd in one,
Against the whore of Babylon.   910
And though those nations be but poor,
Rich kings who fornicate the whore,
Shall melt before them as the snaw,
When rain and south wind makes a thaw.
What men they are he will not clatter,
Lest some think he intends to flatter.
Then all shall be serene and clear,
And saints shall reign a thousand year:
If not, let it not be forgotten,
To hang him when he's dead and rotten. 920
    All doubt much of the Jews conversion,
The manner of the world's eversion.
If fire shall burn the heav'ns to embers?
If sep'rate souls their friends remembers?
If those new reasons do make good
The circulation of the blood?
If webs of cloth be made of stones?
If pox can be chas'd from the bones?
If minerals nourish as grain?
If rats once dead can live again?   930
And of such like resurrections.
If by attractions and ejections,
Men may lend or borrow blood?
If universal drugs be good?
If satire-makers ever thrive?
If any thing which they contrive?

THE WHIGS SUPPLICATION.

If there be fuch of any nation
Who are not driv'n to defperation,
Giving to all who them defends
Still foreft on the finger ends?   940
Though never wifer man was born,
He knows not how to dine the morn,
No more than he fees when fhall come
The moment of the day of doom.

  The Whigs him circled in a ring,
And he ftood like a nine-pin king:
After a paufe and a cough,
And fundry clawings of his hough,
Upon his tiptoes he arofe,
And with his fingers wip'd his nofe;   950
And cleans'd his fingers on his breeches,
Deliv'ring thofe following fpeeches.

  Hear, O ye remnant of *Ifra'l*,
Who have not bow'd your knees to *Baal*,
For which ye undergo the Crofs,
Ye gold refined from the drofs:
Ye winnow'd corn purg'd from the chaff,
Ye fp'rit of malt drawn from the draff;
Who to the good caufe are no fhame,
Ye covenanters, curds, and cream.   960
Ere one a pater-nofter utter,
Some will turn cheefe, and others butter;
And each will feed his hungry brother,
If we fhall chance to eat each other.

Ye who ſtill pray for theſe who wrong you,
God grant there be no rogues among you,
As arch as any of the nation:
I have caus'd pen a Supplication,
Which muſt be ſent unto the king,
From whom ſome muſt an anſwer bring: 970
I'll read it out that ye may mend it;
And then adviſe by whom to ſend it:
Then anſwered the whole crowd,
Bidding him read it out aloud,
Seeking his lunets forth he farted,
At which they who ſtood neareſt ſtarted;
Thoſe further off took ſuch alarms,
Some cry'd to legs, ſome cry'd to arms,
What was the matter none could think,
Till all of them did ſmell the ſtink.   980
Then having huſh'd their ſhouts and halloos,
He did begin to read as follows.

THE SUPPLICATION.

Sir, though there be but few among us,
Who bids at ev'ry word—*God da⋅n us;*
Though we come not to martial cloſes,
Half gelded, and without our noſes,
As not accuſtom'd to thoſe tricks,
Which hurts mens noſes and their ——:

THE WHIGS SUPPLICATION.

Although we do not rant and swagger,
Nor drink in taverns till we stagger,   990
And then engage in drunken quarrels,
Where wit goes out by tooming barrels:
Where some throw stoups, and others glasses,
Some struggle with the serving-lasses:
Some throw a chandler, some a can,
Some strive to cuckold the *Good-man :*
Some mean their elbow, some their head,
Some cry, alas, their shoulder blade!
And some with spilled drink are dripping,
And some sit on a privy sleeping: 1000
Some do not know at whom they're striking,
And some are busy pockets picking:
Some have their hair with fingers freezed,
And some cry out they're circumcised:
Some have their faces and their throples
All scratched with tobacco stopples:
Some coals with naked swords are hewing,
And some lie in a corner spewing:
And other some get bloody fingers,
By grasping naked knives and whingers,   1010
When they the fray intend to redd,
When it were better they were a-bed:
And some cry, ye disturb the *laird,*
And some cry, fie, bring *Bailie Baird ;*
A man who is obliged much
Unto the war against the Dutch.

At that they call the wench to reckon,
She comes and counts up three for one;
But gains not much though she so trick it,
Beside her loss of burgess ticket.   1020
They tell her they would money borrow,
And come and pay their shot to-morrow:
Their officers the other day,
Had dic'd, and drunk, and whor'd their pay.

    Sir, though we do not play such pranks,
For which we give unto God thanks,
Yet we your loyal subjects are,
To serve you both in peace and war,
With our fortunes and our lives;
But if our conscience and our wives,   1030
By any man be meddled with,
We'll both defend with all our pith.
Sir, our conscience to compel,
Is to force our souls to hell.
If we do good, and think it evil,
In that we more obey the devil,
Than doing ill, which we think good,
If holy writ be understood.

    Sir, we have been sore oppressed,
Our wives and serving-lasses cessed,   1040
Either to give beyond their reach,
Or else to hear some hirelings preach;
Who preach nought else, but rail and rant
Against the holy *Covenant*.

THE WHIGS SUPPLICATION.

And yet its known that the nation
Did take it at their inftigation;
For which, of late, they were fo hearty,
When it was the prevailing party,
That they urg'd ftate as they were wood,
To take fome's means, and others blood: 1050
And others they compell'd to flee,
And hide themfelves beyond the fea;
And that, Sir, for no other reafon,
But anti-covenanting treafon.

   But now, Sir, when the guife doth turn,
They preach nothing but hang, and burn,
And herry all thofe of the nation,
Who do refufe the Declaration:
Perfuading us with tales and fictions,
To take oaths which are contradictions; 1060
Having, for love of worldly pelf,
Firft taken contrair oaths themfelf.

   At the firft, Sir, God be thanked,
We fold cov'ring, fheet, and blanket,
And gowns, and plaids, and petticoats,
Meal and peafe, barley and oats,
Butter and cheefe, and wool fleeces,
For groats and fourty-penny pieces:
Capons and hens, and geefe and pigs,
Oxen and horfe which till'd our riggs; 1070
And which our very hearts pierces,
Mafter Zachary Boyd's verfes:

Dickson's sermons, *Guthrie*'s libels,
Bessie of *Lanark*, and our bibles:
And learn'd religion by tradition,
Which smell of Popish superstition.
To pay our fines we were so willing,
Which was for each fault twenty shilling,
Though we alleg'd for our defence,
It was too much by eighteen-pence.   1080
At last we had no more to give,
Neither knew we how to live.
They felled all our hens and cocks,
And rooted out all our kail stocks,
And cast them o'er the dikes away,
And bid us jeering fast and pray.
Being incensed with such harms,
We were necessitate to arms;
And through the country we did come,
We had far better staid at home: 1090
We did nothing but hunt the glaiks;
For after we had got our paiks,
They took us ev'ry one as prizes,
And condemn'd us in assizes,
To be hang'd up every where,
And fix'd our heads up here and there:
Once dreadful heads, Sir, all did doubt 'em,
They had so mickle wit about them.
And we who scap'd those grievous crosses,
Did hide ourselves in bogs and mosses,   1100

Where we fed on fodden leather,
Mingled with the crops of heather,
Which our hunger to affuage,
We thought moſt favoury pottage.
For drink it was no ſmall matter,
If we got clear, not muddy water;
In which we heartily do wiſh,
There be none who defire to fiſh,
That by the devil's inſtigation,
Brings on us all this tribulation.   1110
When in that cafe we could not ſtand,
We fally, Sir, with fword in hand:
Let men cry, *rebels*, till they grow hoarſe,
We'er ſubjects ne'er a whit the worſe.
Though we prefer you not to God,
Who do fo, Sir, their faith will nod.
If government take changing tours,
They will renounce both you and yours;
As doth appear by fome of late,
When the Ufurper rul'd the ſtate.   1120
They ſtrove, Sir, to be fent apace,
To abjure you in the world's face.
Though fome, Sir, of our duniwaifles
Stood out, like *Eglinton* and *Caſſils*,
And others ſtriving to fit ſtill,
Were forc'd to go againſt their will;
Yet other fome, as all men knows,
Who ſhould be fent, were near to blows,

That is, at very boift'rous words,
Putting their hands upon their fwords,   1130
To make men think that they were ftout,
When it was known the world throughout,
To fight your foes when they were fent,
They always took the bog a-fclent;
And running from the fight by ftealth,
Would then fit down and drink your health.
And fince they could not think, like affes,
To beat your foes by drinking glaffes,
Its evident, Sir, as we think,
They drank your health for love of drink. 1140

   Yet many, Sir, were difappointed,
Who fo forfook the *Lord's Anointed*.
They were not all alike regarded,
Some well, and fome were ill rewarded:
They who play'd beft with both the hands,
Enrich'd were by their neighbour's lands.
Some from the creditors got refuges,
Some were made clerks, and others judges:
Some fwearing that their ftocks were fpent,
Strove to get down their annual rent: 1150
Detaining, Sir, by that extortion,
The fatherlefs and widow's portion,
Which us'ring fathers lent to lairds,
Who play'd it all at dice and cards;
Which forc'd fome laffes to mifcarriage,
Becaufe they could not get a marriage.

THE WHIGS SUPPLICATION.   55

But among thofe of ftricter life,
The truth-tell colour grew fo rife,
That it marr'd all the charms and graces,
Of thofe that could not paint their faces.   1160
But other fome got mocks and fcorns,
By giving to their landlords horns,
And fpewing claret mull'd with eggs,
Between the Lord Protector's legs,
When they did endeavour to pray
Before him, on a fafting day.
Some *Whally*'s bible did begarie,
By letting flee at it *Canary*,
Taking it up where it lay next,
That they might read on it the text.   1170
When *Cromwell* preach'd with great applaufe,
The revelation of his caufe;
And fome of them empawn'd their cloaks,
And other fome brought home the pox,
Giving foul linens all the wite,
Some turn'd your friends for mere defpite,
Vowing you never to withftand
Again, without fomething in hand;
And fome turn'd ord'nance-forfakers,
Others, for grief of heart turn'd Quakers.   1180
Some in their confcience took remorfe,
Crying, I'm damn'd, till they grew hoarfe,
And made the ftanders by *admira*,
To fee them take the fits of *Spira*.

To bring those troubled souls to peace,
Some reads *Alvarez'* *Helps to Grace* :
Some, *Sanctuary of a Troubled Soul*,
Some cited passages of *Paul*,
Explaining well what he did say:
Some reads on *Mr. Andrew Gray* :   :190
Some told the danger of backsliding,
Some the good of faith abiding :
Some reads the cases of *Richard Binning*,
Some *Ferguson* reads of *Kilwinning* ;
And some them pressed very sore,
To hear a little of *Doctor More*.
But others cry'd, away, and tush
With vipers in a balmy bush,
With blind *pilots* guiding *ferries*,
With *toads* lurking in *strawberries*.   1200
His doctrine of justification
Drives all the court to desperation.
Few there are saved, as we guess,
By their inherent righteousness.
He hath some good among great evils,
He tells of *Bastard* getting devils :
Of their *bodies*, or *vehicles*,
Their *heraldry* and *conventicles*.
Its sport to see his fancy wander
In their male and female gender.   1210
He doth so punctually tell
The whole economy of hell,

That some affirm he is *Puck Harry;*
Some, he hath walked with the fairy.
Though intellectuals be neat,
Though he means well, and is no cheat,
His case is desperate and sad,
For too much learning makes him mad.
We'll read on the *True Convert's Mark,*
Or we will read on *Beffie Clark,*　　　1220
Or else on *Baker's Heav'nly Beam,*
Or on the *Lady Culrofs' Dream;*
Which sundry drunken asses flout,
Not seeing the jew'l within the clout:
Like coxcombs who take no heed,
When they *Gower* or *Chaucer* read.
When they had said and read their fill,
It did not cure the patients ill:
They still cry on, and howl, and mourn,
Their counsels will not serve the turn.　　1230
No comfort at all find they can,
Until a grave and rev'rend man,
Advise them to resist temptation,
With Spanish wine, and fornication.

　　Those rebels also to obey,
Those hirelings ceas'd for you to pray;
Because their stipends, and their living,
Were at the foresaid rebel's giving.
They thought a man a venial sinner,
Who left sworn duty for his dinner:　　1240

Yea, some of them were of opinion,
They might pray for that *devil's minion*.
They would not stick for love of pelf,
To pray, Sir, for the devil himself.
But we in the usurpers faces,
Remember'd you in pray'rs and graces:
And if we had had guns and swords,
Our actions would have back'd our words.
Our fault, Sir, was, for which we moan,
We thought to do it all alone.   1250
Since it was only want of wit,
Since it was a distraction fit,
We pray you, Sir, be no despiser
Of us, whom God has made no wiser.

    Royal Sir, to those our times
Apply'd may be a poet's rhymes,
Who coarsely singeth, ' that a wight,
' Obeying king in wrong or right,
' If that the king to wreck shall go,
' Will in like manner turn his foe.   1260
' But who obey no sinful thing,
' Do still prove constant to their king.'
The rhyme is barbarous and rude;
But, Sir, the saying's rich and good:
In print yet forth it hath not crept,
We have it in a manuscript.
The *Good-man* keeps it as we think,
Behind a dish upon the bink:

THE WHIGS SUPPLICATION.

And yet its thought by many a man,
Moſt worthy of the *Vatican*. 1270
Its worthy, Sir, of your *Saint James*,
That ſtands upon the river *Thames:*
Ye'll not find, ſaying, ſuch another,
Put all their gilded books together;
Though with theſe two you join in one,
The bibliothec of *Preſter John*.
Cauſe pages cry it ſtill before ye,
As *Philip* did *memento mori*.

   Since, then, we arm for conſcience-ſake,
May't pleaſe you, Sir, ſome pity take, 1280
And not by biſhops inſtigation,
Enforce on us the *Declaration;*
Nor make us give beyond our reach,
To keep's from hearing hirelings preach:
Who laſt year preached oaths to take,
And this year preached them to break.
When they have forc'd men to take 'em,
Then, firſt of all, themſelves they break them.
Except God, Sir, their manners mend,
They'll *oath* it to the world's end: 1290
Men either muſt forſwear themſelf,
As oft as they turn coats for pelf;
Or elſe their conſcience is ſo ſcurvy,
They will turn all things topſy-turvy.
And we will give what we can reach,
To keep's from hearing thoſe men preach,

As Achisons, babees, and placks,
Which is enough, Sir, for our packs.
Likewise, in any other thing,
We will obey you as our king.   1300
If ye require it at our hands,
We'll quit to you both lives and lands.
Nothing to fight can us compel,
Except to keep our souls from hell,
Whatever mischief us befal,
Or else *the devil take us all.*
Ye need not, Sir, distrust or fear,
When *outlaw Whigs* do ban or swear;
It doth unto the world appear,
Keeping our oaths hath cost us dear.   1310
We pray God, that your majesty,
And then your royal progeny,
May peace and truth with us defend,
As king unto the world's end.
We, with all duty and respect,
Your gracious answer do expect.

THE WHIGS SUPPLICATION.

A Debate between the Knight and Squire about the mending of the Petition, and who should carry it to the King.

And thus the Supplication ended,
The Squire cry'd out, It should be mended:
Being desir'd to tell the cause,
First with all ten his a—— he claws,   1320
And then his elbow and his head,
Winking a while as he were dead;
And clapping both hands on his snout,
At last his reason tumbled out:
To wit, it did not move to grant
Renewing of the COVENANT.

KNIGHT.

At which the Knight gave such a groan,
As would have rent a heart of stone:
And casting both his eyes to heav'n,
He said, Not though the Earl of *Leven*   1330
Were on our heads, we durst not do it,
Its base to put the king so to it.
It is a most presumptuous thing,
To cross the conscience of a king.
Some honest men did never take it,
Some honest also were who brake it:

But he who breaks't againſt his light,
Let it be wrong, let it be right,
By prophets and apoſtles leave,
We dare aver he is a knave. 1340
On ſingulars we will not harp,
For the apply will be to *Sharp*.
We put down biſhops to our coſt,
Yet two or three ſtill rul'd the roaſt,
Some of which play'd ſuch pranks at home,
As never Pope preſum'd at Rome.
It is the ſimpleſt of all tricks,
To ſuffer fools have chopping-ſticks:
A ſword put in a wood-man's hand,
Breeds mickle trouble to the land. 1350

SQUIRE.

The Squire reply'd, They're ſcarce of news,
Who tells their mother haunted ſtews,
Who on his brother rubs diſgrace,
He ſpits upon his mother's face,
Each *Covenanter* is our brother,
The *Covenant* of all is mother.
Their wit is dull and very groſs,
Who think where gold is there's no droſs:
Where there is corn there may be chaff,
Where there is malt there may be draff: 1360
Thiſtles with corn grow on the riggs,
And rogues may lurk among the *Whigs.*

And friars in Lent may be flesh-eaters,
And *Covenanters* may be *cheaters*,
And weeds grow up with faireft flow'rs,
And fighing fifters may be whores.
As fruit on trees grow, fo grow leaves,
Its certain bifhops may be knaves.
Its known to all the devil may dwell,
In fome of fourteen as of twelve.　　　　1370
To blame a caufe for perfons vices,
Is one of Satan's main devices,
By which he very oft doth make
Well meaning men the truth forfake.
But let us firft the queftion ftate,
Before we enter in debate,
Which of the two fhould bear the fway,
The *mitres*, or the *elders-lay*.

KNIGHT.

The Knight did paufe a pretty while,
Then anfwer'd with a fcornful fmile :　　1380
I tell thee, fool, I think government
Of Church a thing of fmall concernment :
The truth 'tis very hard to find,
It puzzleth the moft learned mind.
Some do the *Prefbyt'ry* conceive
New forg'd by *Calvin* at Geneve :
Some fay he puts to execution,
Paul the Apoftle's inftitution,

Which suffer'd exile and ejection,
The time of *Paul*'s foretold defection.   1390.
Some say since bishops did appear,
Its more than fifteen hundred year:
Some say that then they did begin,
The Pope of Rome to usher in:
That *Paul*'s iniquities, myst'ry working,
Was men then for precedency forking.
Some Presbyterians do conclude,
But bishops say such thoughts delude,
Which comes from brains which have a bee,
Like *Urquhart's trigonometry*.   1400.
Some bishops prove by Scripture phrases,
As by the word γυβιργησις,
How *John* the angels seven did greet,
Why *Paul* did *Titus* leave in *Crete:*
But other some boldly asserts,
Who reason so the text perverts.
Some call the bishops *weather-cocks*,
Who where their heads were turn their *docks*,
Still stout for them who gives them most,
And who will make them rule the roast.   1410
Some say that bishops have been good,
And seal'd the gospel with their blood;
As ready for the truth at call,
As any Whig among us all.
Perhaps a railing, foolish ranter,
Will tell, a bishop covenanter,

An honeſt clergyman will be,
When cable paſſeth needle's eye:
For ſome of ſuch had play'd a pavie,
Though all the cables of the navy   1420
In one, ſhould paſs through needle's eye,
Whigs ſtill would doubt their honeſty.
Some ſay a biſhop covenanter,
If a penitent repenter,
Cauſeth more joy to ſp'rits divine,
Than all the other ninety-nine.
Some father tales upon *King James*,
To ſundry Preſbyterian dames,
That he was forc'd of knaves to make 'em,
For devil an honeſt man would take them. 1430
Some ſay the king gave never leave,
To make a biſhop of a knave.
That thoſe men are evil ſpeakers,
Tax'd by *Jude* ſpiritual Quakers.
That none doth hate nobility,
For Quakers blaming heraldry.
And ſome again are, who compares
Our biſhops unto *baiting bears;*
Who if they be not kept in awe,
They will tear all with teeth and paw: 1440
Yet tractable in ev'ry thing,
If in their ſnout ye put a ring.
And many men again there be,
Who ſay the ſame of Preſbyt'ry.

And some say this, and some say that,
And some affirm—they know not what.
Its grief to see them Scripture vex,
And wrest it like a nose of wax:
And he who is deceived most,
All fathers on the Holy Ghost.   1450
Some quitting prophets and apostles,
Thinks best to plead the cause by *postils:*
And some do dispute by tradition,
Some calls that Popish superstition:
And some affirm that they had rather
Follow a council than a father:
And some affirm no matter whether
They are blind leaders all together.
And since the truth is found by none,
No more than is that turn gold-stone,   1460
Its best, *Sancho*, for ought I see,
To take a pint and then agree.
Let men have bishops at their ease,
And hear what preachers best them please,
If we be freed of *Declaration*,
And of that other great vexation,
We mentioned in our petition,
We'll alter it on no condition:
Then we will serve the king as much
Against the Dane, and French, and Dutch,
As any in his three dominions,   1470
Who hateth us or our opinions.

If he command us we will come,
Like Goths, and scale the walls of Rome,
And bereave Babel's Whore of breath,
Or die the Duke of Bourbon's death.

SQUIRE.

The Squire made many odd grimace
Ere he could speak, like *Balaam*'s ass.
Sometime he wink'd, sometime look'd up,
And running backward like a tupp,   1480
For to return with greater force;
He snorted like a very horse:
One thought upon another tumbled,
One while he grinn'd, another grumbled,
At last like *Cant*, or *Trail*, or *Durie*,
He gave a broadside in a fury:
Looking as he would eat them all,
His words flew out like cannon ball.
The love of pelf comes from the devil,
Its root of all mischief and evil,   1490
It makes lords sup without a candle,
When none can see their knife to handle;
While to bring candles servants lingers,
Ten candles will not heal their fingers.
It makes foreheads and shins to bleed,
By saving candle to light to bed.
It makes them keep their cellar keys,
Set secret marks on hams and cheese,

Which if but in the leaſt defaced,
Wives, ſervants, bairns, are all menaced.   1500
It makes them prigg for milk and eggs,
Put in their broth cocks halfs' and legs:
It makes them patch elbows and breaſts,
Keep rinded butter in charter cheſts,
Till rats eat all their law defences,
And families old evidences.
It makes them pay their maſons wages
By uſury, on weeds, and gages,
Taken from widows who were plunder'd,
By paying forty in the hundred.   1510
It corrupts *Hamell*, *Sharp*, and *Sweet*,
It poiſons all like *aconite*.
If it touch hide it goes to heart,
And ſo affecteth ev'ry part,
The great ones do betray their truſt,
Ladies throw honour in the duſt,
Like thoſe who trode the Cyprian dance
With that *financier* of France.
It *Puritans* does make of *Ranters*,
And *cavaliers* of *Covenanters*:   1520
Of *lords* and *earls* it makes *drapers*,
Of *prieſts* and *Levites* it makes *capers*.
It makes grave and reverend *cheats*,
In pulpits and tribunal ſeats:
For any crime it finds defences,
With oaths it like a Pope diſpenſes.

It caufes among brethren ftrife,
It makes a man pimp to his wife:
It makes yields fortreffes and towns,
Sooner than armies with great guns :   1530
It fets a-fire cities and ftreets,
It raifes tragedies in fleets :
It makes the vanquifhed victorious,
And foil than victory more glorious :
It makes rebellion rife and fall,
And hath fuch influence on all,
That whom it made rebellious nurfes,
It loyal makes—to fill their purfes.
It caufeth many a bloody ftrife,
When needy male-contents grow rife.   1540
Then by it church and ftate are mended,
And will be till the world be ended.
Mafter, we all obferve and mark,
Since ye once doubt ye will embark,
Why do ye confcience fo neglect?
Or what, Mafter, can ye expect?
Although among the Whigs ye preach,
A bifhopric ye cannot reach ;
For bifhoprics are given to none
Like Prefbyterian *John Gillon*,   1550
Who when he takes his preaching turn,
Will make more laugh than he makes mourn.
Ye have infus'd in us fedition,
Ye will us leave in that condition,

And then cause print a *book of Seaſon*,
Tax whom ye have ſeduc'd of treaſon;
And when ſo doing, all men ſee
Ye ſing the *palinode* of *Lee*,
The cavaliers will ſtill you call
The archeſt rebel of us all. 1560
Thus having ſaid he made a halt,
And ſtood like *Lot*'s wife turn'd to ſalt,
With ear attentive, earneſt eye,
He did expect the Knight's reply.

KNIGHT.

Who ſtroak'd his beard and bit his lip,
And wip'd his noſe and ſcratch'd his hip,
He wry'd his face and knit his brows,
He changed more than twenty hues:
His hands did tremble, his teeth did chatter,
His eyes turn'd up, his bum did clatter, 1570
His tongue on teeth and gums did hammer,
He fain would ſpeak, but ſtill did ſtammer:
His garb was ſtrange, dreadful, uncouth,
Till through his epileptic mouth,
Thoſe following ſpeeches fierce and loud,
Burſt out like thunder through a cloud.
Thou poiſons all my little *Grex*,
Thou ſentence-ſpeaking *Carnifex*,
Thou hardy and preſumptuous are,
To meddle ſo with peace and war: 1580

Rub my horse belly and his coots,
And when I get them—dight my boots,
For they are better than gramashes
For me, who through the dubs so plashes:
Yet I'll wear none, till I put on
Those of the priest of Livingston,
Who when they hid them in the riggs,
Said they were plunder'd by the Whigs:
Unto another priest his marrow,
Who sent a maid his boots to borrow, 1590
Whose boots were plundered indeed,
As was his salt beef and his steed.
Teach what I please, thou'lt not forbear,
To meddle with things without thy sphere,
Like tailors making boots or shoes,
Or like shoemakers making hose:
Like some I know as blind as owls,
Playing at tennis and at bowls,
And sometime shooting at a mark,
Like *Passavantius* playing the clerk, 1600
Who meddled with—he knew not what,
That he might get from Rome a hat.
Men oft by change of station tines,
Good lawyers may prove bad divines.
Like *Sodoleto*'s dog in sattin,
Like *Ignoramus* speaking Latin,
Which raised most unnatural jars,
As between law and gospel wars.

Like *Bembo*'s parrot finging maffes,
Like men of feventy courting laffes,   1610
Like Highland ladies knoping fpeeches,
When they are fcolding for the breeches:
Like *Maffanello* freeing Naples
From *gabels* put on roots and apples:
Like tailors fcanning ftate-concernments,
Or coblers clouting church-governments:
Like fome attempting tricks in *flatics*,
Not vers'd in *Euclid*'s mathematics:
Like piper's mending *Morley*'s mufic,
Or gard'ners *Paracelfus*' phyfic: 1620
Like atheifts pleading law refuges,
Like country tryfters turning judges,
Like preachers ftirring up devotions,
By preaching military motions;
Proving their ufes and *didactics*,
By paffages of *Ælian's tactics*:
Like ladies making water ftanding,
Like young lairds horfe and foot commanding,
Like monkeys playing on a fiddle,
Or eunuchs on a lady's middle: 1630
Like gilliwetfoots purging ftates
By papers thrown in pocks or hats;
That they might be, when purg'd from dung,
Secretaries for the Irifh tongue.
Great wounds yet curable ftill fefter,
When fools prefume to rule their mafter;

As fad experience teach'd of late,
When fuch reformed church and ftate;
Though all the public did pretend,
All almoft had a private end.   1640
There was no place of war or ftate,
But was by twenty aimed at:
Whereof nineteen were difappointed,
Which made the body whole disjointed,
And rais'd among them fuch divifions,
That they were to their friends derifions.
Some aim'd at the *embroider'd purfe*,
Some the *finances* to *deburfe*,
And other fome thought to be getters,
By writing of the *privy* letters: 1650
Some aim'd at privy feal or rolls,
Some cuftoms gather'd in, and tolls:
Some did dry quarterings enforce,
Some lodg'd in pockets foot and horfe;
Yet ftill bog-fclented when they yoked,
For all the garrifon in their pocket:
And fome made men mortgage their lands,
To lend money on public bands,
To be paid at the refurrection:
Some fines paid who oppos'd defection: 1660
Some fold the foldiers mity meal,
And fome did from the public fteal;
And fome, as every body fays,
Us'd more than other twenty ways;

G

Yet notwithstanding of all that,
They were lean kine devouring fat.
None gained by those bloody fairds,
But two three beggars which turn'd lairds;
Who stealing public geese and wedders,
Were freed by rend'ring skin and feathers,
When others of this church and nation   1671
Return unto their former station:
And now, for all their stomach's stout,
Comes home more fools than they went out.
Thou, like a firebrand, dost advise
Us to be fools when all are wise.
Thy endeavours are all in vain.
Ere we shall play such pranks again,
The Patagons shall masses mumble,
The dons of Spain shall all be humble;   1680
Italians shall speak as they think,
Germans, when sun's set, shall not drink;
Swedes gaining day shall not pile baggage,
And English hate shall beef and cabbage;
The Russ and Pole shall never jar,
Danes shall gain by a Swedish war;
Victorious Turk shall stand to reason,
Scots shall be beat, and not blame treason;
The Dutch shall brandy slight, and butter,
And England conquer by De Ruyter;   1690
The first burnt ardour of French hearts
Shall not turn to a crack of farts;

And they shall spell as they do speak,
And they shall sing as they do prick:
With oaths they shall not lard their speeches,
Nor change the fashion of their breeches.
All shall have for assured news,
The Pope from Rome has banish'd stews:
Rebellion shall return from hell,
And do things which I will not tell.   1700
Though it were true as some compares,
Our bishops unto baiting bears,
Who if they be not kept in awe,
They will tear all with teeth and paw,
Yet many utterly mislikes,
That butcher Presbyterian tykes
Should flee upon their throats and faces,
To curb their lordships and their graces:
His majesty without all doubt,
Should only ring them in the snout.   1710
If they so swell that none can bide
Their malice, avarice, and pride,
Vices which all the world doth ken,
Familiar to clergymen;
Of which though palliate with art,
Our Presbyterians had their part:
Our duty is, with all submission,
To press the grant of our petition,
The king will suffer us, perchance,
As Lewis doth Hugonots in France,   1720

And in his wars, civil and foreign,
Make me command in chief, like *Turrain*.
And though he grant not our demands,
Away with *covenants* and *bands*;
Kings muſt command, we muſt obey,
They rebels are who truth gainſay.
Some tell we muſt the truth ſo love,
As of it not to quit a hoof;
As ſaid another fool thy marrow,
As if his majeſty were *Phar'oh*. 1730
For my part ere I trouble peace,
I'll biſhops call, *My Lord and Grace*,
And kneel at the communion-table,
Make Chriſtmas-feaſts if I be able:
Private ſacraments I'll avow,
Childrens confirming I'll allow;
And I will hear the organs play,
And *Amen* to the ſervice ſay.
I'll ſurplice wear, and high-ſleev'd gown,
And to the altar I'll bow down: 1740
Yea, ere his majeſty be wroth,
I'll *primate* be, and *chanc'lor* both.

SQUIRE.

The Squire replied in a chaff,
He grinn'd ſo that he ſeem'd to laugh:
And when ye travel in caroſſes,
Ye will ſalute the highway croſſes;

And when with danger ye are preft,
Ye will crofs, fign forehead and breaft;
And ye will to our lady pray,
And travel on the fabbath-day; 1750
And ye will play with lords and lairds
All fermon-time, at dice and cards,
And duels fight like thofe of France,
And drunk and cripple lead a dance;
And ye will venture axe and rope,
By writing letters to the Pope,
To tell him, though ye here be *Haman*,
Ye worfhip with the king like *Naman*;
And then accufe us all of treafon,
When ye put out your *Book of Seafon*. 1760

KNIGHT.

The Knight look'd fiercely then about,
Thus thund'ring with a dreadful fhout:
Conftant madnefs thy brains enthrals,
Thou haft no lucid intervals;
Thy wafpifh tongue will never fail
To prat, to fcold, revile, and rail,
Though men fhou'd bray thee all to powder,
Thou ftill *Therifles* plays the louder:
All honeft and unbiafs'd, ken
Thofe men whom thou mean'ft were worthy men;
They had fome faults, though not fo big 1771
As rotten flies, to fpoil a pig.

Of ointment; sooner, it is known,
We others faults see than our own:
Presbyterian, never one,
Faultless, at them could cast a stone.
Its certain it comes from the devil,
To hide mens good, and tell their evil:
They never learned that of *Paul,*
Or *David,* when he mourn'd for *Saul.*   1780
Thou art a coxcomb void of reason,
To tell me of a *Book of Season:*
Thou learn'd'st when thou kept sheep and hogs,
With one stone for to hit two dogs:
Though thou spew venom like a toad,
That book is much esteem'd abroad.

SQUIRE.

The Squire replied; Many deem
Beyond sea it is in esteem:
When once it passed Pentland firth,
It rais'd among them such a mirth,   1790
That some for laughter burst their reins,
And other some did split their spleens:
They cherish'd it in ev'ry school,
To be their *Bibliotheca*'s fool.
When serious reading health did spill,
That they might read and laugh their fill,
Physicians it prescrib'd to men
As cure approved for the spleen.

At public meetings and at feasts,
It was the topic of their jests.   1800
Some say, since known, all his life
To have had with the bishops strife;
Since for the cov'nant none more wood,
To make three nations swim in blood;
Since he spar'd none whom he could reach,
Who 'gainst th' *engagement* did not preach;
Since to the cause he stuck so fast,
Since bishops was restor'd at last;
That in the pulpit he did grant
A bishop was the devil's plant,   1810
Giving to all his hearers leave,
If e'er he turn'd, to call him knave.
And since, as ev'ry body says,
He chang'd in less than twenty days,
Its very like, at others budding,
He turn'd his coat for cake and pudding.
Some say he is a sounding brass,
Which signifies a prattling ass:
He brings no reason which can bind,
But only fights against the wind.   1820
Its clear that it doth with him fare,
As with *Sampson* without his hair.
Before his change his wit was tough,
And he could reason well enough:
But now he kytheth like a fool,
As one would whip a boy at school,

To vent in print so little reason,
And call it an Advice in season.
Some say that he treads bishops path,
As *David* serv'd the king of Gath.   1830
'Though men to censure him be rash,
He gives the bishops such a dash,
They need not brag their cause is won
By the foster of *Henderson*.
Some say he bishops doth betray;
That Presbyt'ry may gain the day,
Who fed him for their champion hidden;
Others affirm they are outbidden,
Which makes him take a contrair task,
As Edward answer'd once Southesk.   1840
A modest man wrote in a letter,
He might have pleaded mickle better.
The charitable do not fear;
But for a thousand merks a year
He would the bishops yet withstand,
If covenanters rul'd the land.

KNIGHT.

Then said the Knight; Though in a mortar
I bray this fool, to no exhorter
Thou wilt give ear; he'll put thee to it.

SQUIRE.

To whom the Squire; What though he do it;

THE WHIGS SUPPLICATION.

Both reaſon there and juſtice halts, 1851
Where one's blam'd for another's faults.
Was never judge did things ſo foul,
Except himſelf once at St. Rule:
He forg'd records, and them enacted,
To bear falſe witneſs when extracted.
I cannot tell till I adviſe,
Whether he did it twice or thrice.
Next I will tell that he gave leave,
If e'er he turn'd, to call him knave: 1860
But he can challenge no reflection
Put on him at his own direction.
He is oblig'd to keep his word
As well as one who wears a ſword:
But if he chance to be ſo wroth,
As to break word as well as oath,
I'll tell him I take frantic fits,
And am diſtracted of my wits,
As he and others ſaid of late,
When they miſguided church and ſtate. 1870
And I them tax'd of forg'd records,
As I can prove before the lords.
If that ſucceed not, it effeers
That I be judged by my peers;
That is, by fifteen poetaſters,
Half fools, half beggars, half burleſquers:
All of them proved drinkers, whorers,
By preachers, forgers, and perjurers.

Ere such a jury can be gotten,
Its certain I'll be dead and rotten ;   1880
Or if, justice so shall halt,
As to cause hang me for this fault,
Hanging to me will be less trouble,
Than worry on a windy bubble
At a dike side, or under a stair,
If weather be not very fair.

KNIGHT.

But then the Knight; We'll hear he'll quarrel,
That thou once served Albemarle.

SQUIRE.

To which the Squire, I have no fears,
He dare not challenge't for his ears ;   1890
For I can make appear to all
They tofs'd me to him like a ball.
Next, ask that duke, in any thing
If e'er I did prejudge the king.
I forc'd was to dissimulation,
To shun a rope, and serve my nation.
I did no evil but mickle good,
Saving mens money and their blood ;
Which services I did for nought,
Which were from men far richer bought.   1900
That duke can tell he did suspect it,
Albeit to try he did neglect it,

When by their crafty inftigation,
He urg'd was to my accufation.
They all now tell of Albemarle,
But they told him another quarrel,
In pleading I could touch a ftring,
Whofe found will make their ears to ring.

KNIGHT.

The Knight faid, Tufh, they'll no more ftir,
Than moon when bark'd at by a cur: 1910
For all thy prat, on no condition
I mind to alter the petition.

SQUIRE.

Then faid the Squire ; If ye'll not mend it,
Advife, at leaft, by whom to fend it.
Since we petition for religion,
Your lady, or your dog, or pigeon,
Were fitteft to be fent : if other,
I'm fore afraid we lofe a brother ;
For I dare fwear upon th' evangel,
When he hath got from each his *angel*, 1920
To help his charges to defray,
The fellow will us all betray.

KNIGHT.

When things fucceed not, fools do flite,
Giving betraying all the wite,

Reply'd the Knight; they said of late,
They were betray'd when they were beat;
And they said true; who did not stand,
Betrayed are by heart and hand.
But to the point; as for my wife,
I'll never send her in my life,　　　　　　1930
For fear some courtier or other,
Would make me old *King Arthur*'s brother.
My dog is an unruly cur,
And at the court will keep a stir;
Seeing *Conformists* up and down,
He barks so at a high-sleev'd gown,
That bishops either will cause stone him,
Or else yoke butcher dogs upon him.
As for my pigeon it cannot be,
She hath another gate to flee:　　　　　　1940
A message she hath tane in hand,
To search for that most happy land,
Unknown to any heretofore,
But only to *Sir Thomas More*,
Where we intend to fix plantation,
If forc'd to change our habitation.
And since a poet rightly hits,
That greatest fools have greatest wits,
To shun false dealing, it is fit
To choose one not o'ergrown in wit:　　　1950
So he can buffonize and jest,
At public meeting and at feast,

THE WHIGS SUPPLICATION.

And catch a time to tell the truth,
Like *David*'s great-grandmother *Ruth*.
The Whigs with an applauding halloo,
Cry'd out his counsel they would follow;
Which once concluded, all arose,
And set on pans to make their *brose*.
When after that some fools were nam'd
To be employ'd, they all were blam'd;
And none thought fit' they still inquire,
And find none fitter than the Squire.
On him then they enforc'd the message.
When he went out on his embassage,
How at the court he did arrive,
How to affront him they did strive:
But how the buffoons all he outed,
How *Hudibras*'s squire he routed,
When they two yoked by the ears
About the baiting of the bears:
And how he manag'd every thing,
And how he did harangue the king;
And how he cited ends of verse,
And sayings of philosophers;
At which some laugh'd, and some were vex'd,
Ye'll be advertis'd by the next.

NOTES.

Ver. 32. Plack, *one third of a penny.*

V. 35. Tafs, *the famous Torquato Taffo, an Italian poet, born at Sorrento in Naples. His works are,* Jerusalem Delivered; *and* Amintas, *a Pastoral Comedy. He died in 1595, being about to receive the degree of Poet Laureat.*

V. 36. Marine, *John Baptifta Marina, a famous poet, born at Naples about the middle of the 16th century.*

V. 77. Garvie fifhes, *fprats.*

V. 92. Caput Bonae Spei, *the Cape of Good Hope.*

V. 96. Riggs, *ridges.*

V. 97. Hoggars, *coarfe hofe, wanting feet.*

V. 98. Coots, *ankles.*

V. 99. Durks, *daggers.*

V. 105. Ratches, *firelocks.*

V. 106. Peats, *turff.*

V. 112. Dalzel, *general to King Charles II. at the battle of Pentland hills in 1666, where the king's army was victorious.*

Ibid. His paiks; *that is, to drub him.*

V. 143. Groff, *intelligible.*

V. 175. Barrow-trams, *the poles of a hand-barrow.*

V. 176. Reifted hams, *fmoked bacon.*

V. 182. Penny-bridle, *a paying wedding.*

Ver. 186. Spinola besieg'd Breda. *This was in 1624, with 39,600 men. His entrenchments were 30,600 paces in compass. Spinola understanding, by letters of Prince Maurice which were intercepted, that vast preparations were making to raise the siege, though in the cold of winter, he raised a trench of 52,000 paces in compass, to defend his camp. The town was obliged to surrender to him on the 5th of June, 1625.*

V. 190. Brose, *water-gruel.*

V. 257. Gramash, *spatterdash.*

V. 258. Panash, *feather.*

V. 262. Bannockburn, *a little village of Scotland, within two miles of Stirling, where, in 1313, in the reign of Edward II. of England, and Robert Bruce of Scotland, the English army, commanded by Edward, was defeated by the Scots.*

V. 274. Saddle tore, *saddle bow.*

V. 284. Ariosto, *an Italian poet; author of the* Orlando Furioso. *He died in 1533.*

V. 287. Tine, *lose.*

V. 296. Coutchers, *clowns.*

V. 330. Sodds, *pack saddle.*

V. 346. John Thomson's man; *a hen-peck'd fellow.*

V. 350. Pose, *purse.*

V. 372. Declaration. *All who were in any public employment were to take that oath, by the 5th act of the 2d sess. of the 1st parl. of Charles II. in 1661; by which they acknowledged it was unlawful to take up* arms against the king; as also that the national Solemn League and Covenant were not binding upon the nation.

Ver. 398. *Monsieur did Agrippa's dog.* *Wierus says, there was a report, though false, of Agrippa, that he had two devils in the shape of dogs; the one called Monsieur, and the other Mademoiselle; to one of which he said at his death, 'Get you gone you wretched beast, 'who hath destroyed me.' Upon which it ran into the river, and was never seen afterwards.*

V. 404. Fish, whose liver frights the devil. *We have the account of that fish in* Tobit, *chap. iv. ver. 7. where the angel gives the recipe of driving away devils by its smoke, in chap. viii. ver. 3. Tobias, at his marriage with Sarah the daughter of Raguel, dispersed the bill; and immediately upon smelling that smoke, the evil spirit fled from the river Tigris to the utmost bounds of Egypt.*

V. 413. Carl, *churl.*

V. 449. Rife, *frequent.*

V. 501. Prester John, *the Emperor of Abyssinia.*

V. 514. Flodden, *a place in Northumberland, famous for the defeat of the Scots army by the English, under the command of the Earl of Surrey, in* 1513. *It was uncertain whether James the Fourth was slain in the field of battle or not.*

V. 654. Lawings, *reckonings.*

V. 709. Ripples, *a weakness in the back and reins.*

V. 730. Horse-coupers, *jockeys.*

NOTES.

Ver. 763. Jove has his guard, *that is, Satellites Jovis.*

V. 895. Pomer into Scluse. *From Pomerania, a country of Germany on the Baltic, to Dutch Flanders.*

V. 904. Italian voyage. *He means the Sicilian Vespres, on Easter Eve, 1382, when the Sicilians massacred all the French in the island..*

V. 975. Lunets, *pockets.*

V. 992. Tooming, *emptying.*

V. 993. Stoups, *pots.*

V. 1005. Throples, *throats.*

V. 1011. The fray intend to redd; *to end the squabble.*

V. 1020. Burgess ticket, *maidenhead.*

V. 1049. Wood, *mad.*

V. 1057. Herry, *impoverish.*

V. 1068. Fourty-penny pieces, *three-pence, and one third of a penny.*

V. 1072. Master Zachary Boyd's verses. *He was a poet. He paraphrased or rather burlesqued several places of Scripture: probably that was owing more to ignorance than design.*

V. 1074. Bessie of Lanark. *This is a small pamphlet, by way of dialogue betwixt a minister and her.*

V. 1084. Kail, *cabbage.*

V. 1091. Hunt the glaiks, *go of a fool's errand.*

V. 1102. Crops of heather, *tops of heath.*

V. 1123. Duniwaisles, *highland gentlemen.*

V. 1134. Took the bog a-sclent; *they fled.*

NOTES.

Ver. 1167. Begarie, *bespatter.*

V. 1175. Wite, *blame.*

V. 1184. Spira. *He died in despair, blaspheming God.*

V. 1222. Lady Culross' dream. *She was his own mother: That dream was a sort of trance of hers as she imagined: The author published it.*

V. 1242. Devil's minion, *Oliver Cromwell.*

V. 1268. Bink, *cupboard.*

V. 1284. Hirelings, *Episcopal ministers.*

V. 1297. Achison, *two thirds of a penny; so called from one Achison, master of the mint in Scotland.*

Ibid. Babee, *one half of a penny.*

V. 1298. Packs, *flocks.*

V. 1308. Ban, *curse.*

V. 1330. The Earl of Leven. *He was a general, and a very great soldier.*

V. 1396. Forking, *striving.*

V. 1476. Duke of Bourbon. *He was general to Charles V. He led an army against Rome, and besieged the Pope.*

V. 1480. Tupp, *a ram.*

V. 1485. Cant, Trail, or Durie; *three famous Presbyterian ministers.*

V. 1501. Prigg, *to cheapen.*

V. 1502. Halss, *throat.*

V. 1504. Rinded, *melted.*

V. 1589. Marrow, *companion.*

V. 1605. Sodoleto. *He was a very learned cardinal. He was bishop of Carpentras, and in great esteem for his learning with Pope Leo. X. Clement VII. and Paul III. He died in* 1547.

Ver. 1609. Bembo's parrot. *This was Cardinal Bembo, famous for his poetry and the elegancy of his style. He was secretary to Leo X.*

V. 1611. Knoping speeches, *pretending to speak finely.*

V. 1622. Country trysters, *referees, who compose differences among neighbours.*

V. 1631. Gilliwetfoots, *the attendants on highland chieftains.*

V. 1706. Tykes, *dogs.*

V. 1745. Carosses, *coaches.*

V. 1769. Ken, *know.*

V. 1772. Pig, *pot.*

V. 1806. The engagement; *called also the Duke's engagement, because the Duke of Hamilton headed the Scots army, which entered England the middle of June,* 1648. *They were routed at Preston in Lancashire by Cromwell's army.*

V. 1815. Budding, *bribing.*

V. 1825. Kytheth, *appears.*

V. 1854. St. Rule, *the name of a place.*

V. 1873. Effeers, *appears.*

V. 1888. Albemarle, *General Monk.*

V. 1923. Flite, *scold.*

V. 1944. Sir Thomas More, *viz. his utopia.*

V. 1968. Hudibras's Squire, *viz. Ralph the sectary.*

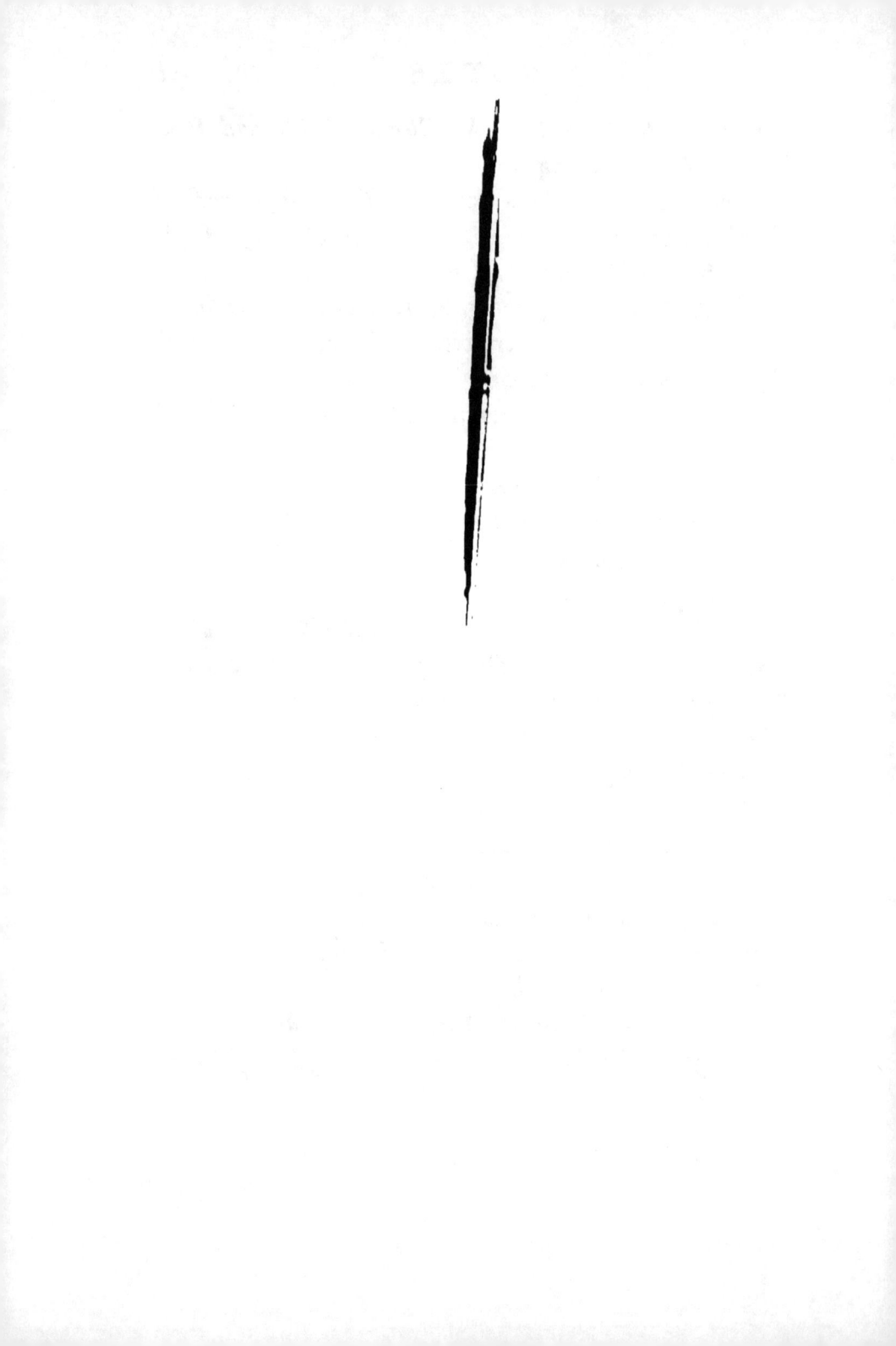

THE WHIGS SUPPLICATION.

A

MOCK POEM.

PART II.

WHEN bushes budded and trees did chip,
And lambs by sun's approach did skip;
When mires grew hard like toasted bread,
That men might through the carses ride;
When folks drew blood of arms and legs,
When geese and turkeys hatched eggs;
When poor folks pots were fill'd with nettles,
When fish did domineer in kettles;
When Lent did fore annoy the glutton,
When sun left *fish* to lodge with *mutton*; 10
When night and day were of like length,
Of March the eighth, or twelfth, or tenth;
When sev'ral critics great and small,
By mending lines did mar them all;

THE WHIGS SUPPLICATION.

When tranfcribers prepoft'rous fpeed,
Made them like pictures fpoil'd with thread,
On arras hangings back-fide ; when
The low'r'd miftakings of fome men
Made fev'ral great wits of the land.
Blame what they did not underftand ; 20
And fome to hunt a flea contrive ;
The Squire near London did arrive.
To meet him old and young came forth,
As Rome did once to fee *Jugurth*.
They knew each paffage of his journal,
Both by report and by diurnal.
We dread they will him fore abufe,
But let us firft invoke the mufe.

   Thou, Mufe, who never doft abandon
Thofe who have fcarce a leg to ftand on, 30
When they afcend Parnaffus' mountain,
Till in the end they tafte a fountain,
Which makes them than an owl fing fweeter ;
Make me once more a fool in metre,
That I may be of all admired,
Confuting Prefbyt'ry cafhiered,
Which I of late fo much adored :
But now when I get nothing for it,
Make me, O Mufe, to change my note,
Declare againft it, turn my coat : 40
Compefce me, Mufe, thefe ftout bravadoes,
Of thefe ftiff-necked reformadoes,

Who still maintain unto this day,
They've the office though they want pay;
In others harvest putting their sickles,
Troubling the land with conventicles,
Whose stubborn hearts cannot be turned
By the Dialogues of *Gilbert Burnet*.
Prove, Muse, that synod-men, church-wardens
Are bears, and synods are bear-gardens; 50
For both have tongues, and teeth, and nails,
But, Muse, what wilt thou do for tails?
But that's all one the matter's small,
For true bears have no tails at all;
And so the simile still jumps,
Instead of tails thou'lt find there rumps.
When thou show'st how the Squire disputed,
And Ralph the sectary confuted,
That he of wits almost bereft him:
But to the Squire now where we left him. 60
   He melted all in tears for pity,
Seeing the ruins of the city:
But when he saw in other places
Houses arise with goodly faces,
And turrets mounting up and soaring,
And the air's middle region boring,
(So *Phœnix* when its burnt in spices,
Up starts another from its ashes,)
Cry'd out the Squire, *Rome* once was burn'd,
By *French* then world's mistress turn'd; 70

God may the same to London grant,
If it renew the COVENANT.
While this he spoke his horse he lights off,
And with his handkerchief he dights off
Tears from his eyes; then on the ground
He grov'ling lies meditabound.
His horse's grievous succussation
Had so excoriate his foundation,
That, till the hide his hips did come on,
The earth he could not set his bum on. 80
Then after sad ejaculations,
He vents these following meditations.
 Wallace, quoth he, having ado,
Still eat the quarter of a cow,
And to the boot ere clothes were put on,
He would sometimes dispatch a mutton;
For when he wanted morning fare,
He was like *Sampson* without hair.
A priest whose teeth did head and legs swell,
Did still eat powder'd beef and eggs twell 90
Before he preach'd, else he half dumb sings,
Like to a fiddle wanting some strings.
Hence by experience I gather,
He is a liar though my father,
Who thinks a man can do or speak well,
Who doth neglect his fast to break well.
I am engag'd in a transaction,
Quoth he, requiring tongue and action,

That to my tackling I may faſt ſtick,
Though I ſhould loſe my ears like *Baſtwick:*
Though they ſhould tie me heel and neck faſt,
Its requiſite I take my breakfaſt.
  This ſaid, his budget he unlooſeth,
And all the wealth within diſcloſeth,
Which for variety did ſcorn
The wealthy *Amalthea's horn;*
Or the rich abbey of *St. Lawrence,*
Or cabin of the *Duke* of *Florence;*
Juſt like the pocks of *Graham* and *Guthry,*
It was his *veſtry* and his *buttry,*
His *larder* and his *bibliothec.*
There lies of oat-meal near a peck,
With water's help which girdles hot bakes,
And turns to bannocks and to oat cakes:
There a piece beef, there a piece cheeſe lies,
And there an old night cap of frieze lies,
His head attire when he the houſe keeps,
On which now here and there a louſe creeps;
Here lies a pair of ſhoes ne'er put on,
And there lies a poor man of mutton:
There lies half dozen ells of pig-tail,
There his panaſh, a capon's big tail,
With white in middle ſhining ſtar-like,
And there be onion heads and garlic,
The food of Turkiſh janizaries:
There turpentine and larie berries,

His medicine for paſſage ſweer,
That for the van, theſe for the rear:
And there a piece of powder'd fiſh lies,
And there ſome butter in a diſh lies: 130
There turnips thirty inch about lies,
And there ſome pepper in a clout lies:
There Fingram ſtockings ſpun on rocks lies,
And there his ſneezing mill and box lies:
There lies his elſon and his lingle,
Which double-ſol'd ſhoes makes of ſingle,
With help of old pieces of leather:
There lies ſome wool that he did gather,
Left by the ſheep as certain pledges
They were entangled in the hedges: 140
There clouts and papers little mugs ſtops,
As in apothecaries drug ſhops,
With vinegar and oil for ſallads:
And there lies books, and here lies ballads;
As *Davie Lindſay*, and *Gray Steel*,
Squire Meldrum, *Bewis*, and *Adam Bell*:
There *Bruce* and *Wallace*, fierce-like Mars knights,
There lies *dialogues* which his arſe dights:
There *Laſt Good Night*, and *Chevy Chaſe*,
With *Gens d' Arms* in the frontiſpiece, 150
Which makes more weep when they read on it,
Than curates ſermons, fie upon it!
And there lies bands, ſhirts, and cravats,
There two three ſkins of lambs and rabbits,

THE WHIGS SUPPLICATION.

For to commence a London trade,
And this was all the wealth he had.
But pardon me, I had forgot,
There was some other thing I wot,
I think it powder was and lead,
To shoot the bishop through the head.   160
    He takes a bible with cov'ring worn off,
And ending and beginning torn off,
He reads, and then he says the grace,
Then to his victuals falls apace.
When first bit scarce down throat was sliding,
Within a day's march of the midding,
Then he a multitude espies,
Approaching him with shouts and cries:
He leaves his victuals, falls a-gazing,
Just like a tupp when he's a-grazing.   170
When folks come by he slights his food,
Stares in their face and chews his cud.
He thought these fools came out to meet him,
That first they might salute and greet him,
That afterwards they might him bring
With greater pomp unto the king:
Such honour at their entry hours,
Are due unto ambassadors.
Both dust and sweat from face he rubs off,
A looking-glass he makes the dubs of: 180
He trims his beard, and then his head too,
Rights basket-hilt on shoulder-blade too;

His hands he wafhes, pairs his nails,
Takes his panafh of capons tails,
Which he pins on before his hat;
He put about a clean cravat;
And then upon his hands he ftretches
Two yellow gloves, with green filk ftitches;
Leaps to his horfe, and on he went,
To take and give the compliment,   190
While hips excoriate made him fwaddle
Through all the corners of the faddle.

When he the multitude approaches,
His eyes he fix'd firft on the coaches,
Ranged like wild-geefe in a line;
Then cry'd he out, no friend of mine,
If I can hinder, thofe fhall enter.
'Tis wonder people fo fhould venture,
To break their arms, and legs, and heads,
And to disjoint their fhoulder blades;   200
Ladies to have their naked breeches
Both view'd and lanced by the leeches,
Which made fome hufbands forth a tuck hold,
Swearing the rogue would make them cuckold.
Thofe made a lady of our land,
Upon her neck and fhoulders ftand,
With a third of half dozen thighs,
Naked erected to the fkies;
And ere that pofture fhe was got off,
Many did fee the thing ye wot of;   210

THE WHIGS SUPPLICATION.

Which when they told her, readily
She anfwered, fhe wonder'd why
They did not kifs't, and take their leave on't,
It was the laft fight they fhould have on't.
She vow'd thereafter, well I wot,
With her grand-dame to walk a-foot:
When coachmen drinks and horfes ftumble,
Its hard to mifs a barla-fumble.
 Then did he ferioufly begin
Well to confider thofe within: 220
He foon perceived by their poftures,
They were no nuns brought up in cloifters.
To fhow their legs fome trufs their laps,
Some throw off fcarfs to fhow their paps;
Some mafked were the fun to keep out,
Which lifting now and then they peep out;
Widows from veils fet out their nofes,
As fnails do from their fhelly houfes;
As they would fay unto the gallants,
Come, gentlemen, behold our talents!   230
Come nearer that we may efpy you,
If ye be ought worth we will buy you;
Where ten to one fome get a fortune,
As one did with my Lady Norton!
 Among the reft he did efpy ones,
Whom he conceived to be he-ones:
Thofe he believed were his mates,
Ambaffadors of kings and ftates,

To do him honour at his entry,
With the nobility and gentry.   240
He cry'd to them to keep the peace,
And not to wrangle for the place;
For all of them remember'd well,
Of that Bowtad of Bateveile,
Which coſt the lives of brave commanders;
And well nigh loſt his maſter Flanders.
He bids them all take place by lots,
No king had place but he of Scots,
Whoſe royal anceſtors 'tis clear,
Has kept one race two thouſand year;   250
Whoſe ſucceſſors as yet eſcaped
The tricks of *Pepin* and *Hugh Capet*.
Others are not of that condition,
They're kings but of a late edition:
Though ſome be ſmall and others greater,
Yet who go firſt or laſt no matter;
For all their gold, ſpices, and wines,
They come from interrupted lines.

    Being inform'd of his miſtake,
It was to ladies that he ſpake: 260
What devil they are! reply'd the Squire,
They're men in garb, and in attire;
They've veſts, they've ſwords, they've periwigs,
They tread the meaſure of the gigs;
Juſt like the men their buttocks vaper,
They caſt their gammonds up and caper;

THE WHIGS SUPPLICATION.

They cajole ladies at the balls too,
And ſtanding piſs againſt the walls too;
They're ſpurr'd and booted when they ride too,
And gallop, when they hunt, aſtride too; 270
With ſwords and piſtols they fight hard too,
Some have appearance of a beard too;
And which of all's the greateſt wonder,
They lie above—their gallants under.
Me's dames, quoth he, that we may ken
Whether ye women be or men,
Its fit ye open keep before
About a trencher breadth or more;
Ye're monſters if that do not meaſure
The circuits of your holes of pleaſure. 280
    While he was giving this advice,
They all ſurround him in a trice:
All wond'ring at his equipage,
Some aſk'd his horſe's price and age?
If there came ſympathetic ſpeed
From rider's heel, or heel of ſteed?
If there came an enchanting force
To maſter's purſe, from ſkin of horſe?
Some, why no ſpurs his ſides to claw,
And for boots ſev'ral ropes of ſtraw? 290
Why ſodds for ſaddle, and branks for bridle,
And plaids for ſcarf about his middle?
Some aſked his panaſh's price?
If 'twas a bird of Paradiſe?

Some ask'd if basket-hilt and dudgeon,
Had ever set a work chirurgeon?
Some jeer'd the long crown of his hat,
Some at his gloves, some his cravat;
Asking more questions at once,
Than would have puzzled *John* of *Duns*, 300
Or *Bonaventure*, or *Socinus*,
Or *Biel*, *Ockam*, or *Aquinas*.
   When *Sinan Bassa* charg'd a hill,
To try his military skill,
Though many a grievous wound it got,
By cannon and by musquet shot,
The hill did neither bow nor bend,
Although he charg'd it thrice on end,
But still abode him face to face,
Choosing to die upon the place, 310
Rather than turn its back and yield;—
Just so the squire did keep the field,
And bravely did receive their tongue-shot,
Just as the hill did *Sinan*'s gun-shot:
He stood as senseless as a stock is,
Or among raging waves a rock is,
When furiously they knock its crown,
To make it break or make it drown.
At last he said with sober grace, 319
When ye grow hoarse ye'll hold your peace.
Then fair and softly on he stripped;
For like a Spaniard when he's whipped,

He thought it was a great difgrace,
For to accelerate his pace.
  When they him faw fo little troubled,
Then they their queftions redoubled:
Some afk'd his errand and his name,
And from what potentate he came?
From Turk, or Sophy, or Mogul,
Who wear much linen on their fkull?   330
Or from either Tartarian Cham,
Who of their horfe' hips make a ham?
Or from Pegu, or from Chine,
Or from th' Emperor of Abyffine?
Or from the Mufcovite or Poll,
Or Dane, whofe chiefeft wealth is toll?
Or from the Emperor or the Swede,
Or Hogen-Mogen brotherhood?
From the Savoyard or the Swifs,
Who apples feethes with roafted geefe?   340
From Florentine or Portuguefe,
Or from Morocco or from Fefs?
Or if he came from Spain or France?
Or from fome Indian Weerowance,
To barter gold and beaver fkins,
For glaffes, beads, and knives and pins?
Or from the Prefbyterian Scots,
Who never yet had turn'd their coats,
Did he a Supplication bring,
To put ill counfel from the king;   350

And that his majesty would grant
Renewing of the COVENANT:
And had commission for to tell him,
If he refus'd they would compel him?
When thus they pressed him so fast,
Patience turn'd Fury at the last:
These last words did him so enrage,
He fac'd about and gave a charge;
Then with his tongue out thus he stutters,
With face awry like old cheese cutters: 360

 You cursed Antichristian rabble,
Ye mongrels of the whore of Babel,
Ye sectaries and cov'nant breakers,
Half cuckold and half cuckold-makers,
For all your flouting and your taunting,
When we went first a-covenanting,
Ye did us court, ye did us bribe,
Invited us like Judah's tribe,
To purge your ten tribes of Isra'l,
From Jeroboam's calf and Baal: 370
Your money mov'd our conscience,
To arm ourselves in your defence.
When our intentions you had got,
And by our means had under foot
Trod all your foes, and them defeated,
At last we found we were but cheated.
Your quarrel was pretended bondage,
By reason of *tunnage* and of *poundage*.

To get *militia* by law,
To keep his majesty in awe, 380
To free yourselves when money waxes,
From inquisitions and taxes:
Your only end was self enriching,
Your sole religion was your kitching;
You valu'd puddings sod in pocks,
More than religion orthodox;
Where as we witness, God and angels,
Prophets, apostles, and evangels,
For trash or any earthly thing,
We never did oppose the king: 390
Yea, all of us, both great and small,
Will quit him lives and lands, and all,
So he give way to purge the temple,
As pleaseth *Mr. Gabriel Semple*.
He spoke so thick, he paus'd a little,
And having cleans'd his beard from spittle,
Like *Tindal* at the stake he cries,
Lord open the King of England's eyes,
And then his majesty will grant
Renewing of the COVENANT. 400
 Thus did he perorate his fliting,
As at Tarentum's spiders biting,
They were affected thereanent,
According to their temperament:
Sanguinians did only laugh,
Choleric Melancholians chaff:

Some bade hang him, some bade stone him,
And some did mastives hunt upon him:
Some *Daple* under tail did prick,
And made him bounce and leap and kick: 410
Some aim'd to tear his straw gramashes,
Some cries have at beard and mustaches:
Some grasped him about the middle,
Till bum did sound like gambo fiddle:
Some would have breeches down to whip him,
Some with their nails would tear and nip him,
Some with briars and thorns would scratch him:
One fearing that they would dispatch him,
Who was a man more moderate,
He made a court'sy with his hat, 420
And begged leave to plead his cause,
According to the nation's laws.

   Contending with a foolish tongue,
Quoth he, is but a war with dung:
Though in the strife we prove victorious,
Dirt makes our finger ends inglorious,
As lately happen'd unto one,
Who needs would quarrel *Sanderson*,
And prove he was a lying knave,
Of which what credit could he have; 430
When he had done he prov'd no more,
Than all the world knew before.
To take such pains imports as much,
As any doubted he were such:

THE WHIGS SUPPLICATION. 109

Refuting such as he with words,
Is like Canary washing t——;
The wine in taste and hue grows meaner,
But t—— grow ne'er a whit the cleaner.
 This simile though somewhat rude,   440
Yet so appeas'd the multitude,
That by degrees their clamour fell,
Like sound of lutestring or of bell,
When thumb or hammer of a clock
Gives the epilogizing stroke:
And in the end these furious criers
Stood silent like *observant friars*,
Or like to dumbies making signs,
Or like to fiddles wanting strings,
Or like to salmons or to cods,
Or Turks when they took in the *Rhodes*.   450
Then piece and piece they dropt away,
As ripe plumbs in a rainy day;
Till in the end they all were gone,
And left him standing all alone.
 Like as we do observe and see,
In those who are condemn'd to die,
That they are sore annoy'd and troubled,
At first when they cast off their doublet,
Truss up their hair, their eyes blindfold,
That they may not grim death behold,   460
Thinking their neck the stroke is hard on,
If any tell them of a pardon:

K

Although their heart be lighted somewhat,
Yet fear and hope still fight a combat,
Till that they hear the air to ring,
With clamours of—' God save the king:'
Then hope triumphs and fear doth vanish,
Like grief when its expell'd by Spanish:—
Just so the Squire, when all at once
They him oppress'd with fists and stones,   470
A gelid fear his heart possess'd,
His final hour approach'd he guess'd;
Trembling he stood in a quandary,
And purg'd as he had eaten laric,
As was confirmed by the speeches
Of those who, after, wash'd his breeches.
When he perceived the retreat,
That flight, quoth he, is but a cheat,
Like that of Greeks, for to destroy
An ancient city called Troy,   480
By help of that tree horse of *Pallas:*
It is some stratagem of *Wallace,*
Who, in a pig-man's weed at Biggar,
Espied all the English leaguer.
But when he found by certain trial,
The retreat was not forg'd, but real,
Then did he resolution show,
And like a cock began to crow.
   One man, quoth he, oft-times hath stood,
And put to flight a multitude,   490

Like *Sampson*, *Wallace*, and *Sir Bewis*,
And *Finmacoul*, beside the *Lewis*,
Who in a bucking time of year,
Did rout and chase a herd of deer,
Till be behind, and they before,
Did run a hundred miles and more,
Which, questionless, prejudg'd his toes,
For *red-shanks* then did wear no shoes;
For to this day they wear but calf ones,
Or, if old leather, half ones.. 500
He chased them so furiously,
That they were forc'd to take the sea;
And swam from Cowel into Arran,
In which soil though it be but barren,
As learned antiquaries say,
Their offspring lives unto this day.
But pardon me for such digressions;
For, were it not for such expressions,
Which from the muses we extort,
Our poems would be very short. 510
 Then did the Squire obtest and pray,
And them conjur'd that they would stay,
For he had quarrel against none,
But *Ralph* the squire, and *Sanderson*;
Which two, as every body knows,
Are Presbyterians mortal foes.
Th' one calls them bears by allegory;
That other fellow wrote a story,.

In which he doth them scandalize so,
That all the devils blush,—he lies so: 520
Thinking it would be liked well,
He sent a copy into hell,
To be perus'd in a committee;
Then said a devil which was witty,
It serves for nothing, tell the fool,
But to be napkins at the stool,
When men exonerate their tripes,
Or lighting of tobacco pipes;
For hell's affairs are ne'er achiev'd
By railing fools, of none believ'd: 530
Hell's fittest agents, as all grants,
Are those who are reputed saints.
And thus he made an end of praying.

   Then all began to think of staying,
And one another did exhort,
For to return and see the sport;
But *Sanderson* appeared not:
Stout *Ralph* affrighted not a jot,
Bravely and resolutely did fall up,
First at the trot, then at the gallop, 540
Just as the Hugonots victorious,
At Courtras charg'd the Duke of Joyeuse,
And was upon him ere he wist,
Menacing him with tongue and fist,
With all the rabble in his rear,
Who followed him to see and hear.

THE WHIGS SUPPLICATION.

   The Squire who only spoke in jest,
Seeing what he expected least,
He thought they verily were gone,
And that the storm was over blown,   550
Surprised with the sudden danger
Of *Ralph* in such a furious anger,
Whom he thought did already spurn him,
He knew not to what hand to turn him:
At last his tongue and teeth commences,
To vent adages and sentences.
   It is a saying wise and old,
Quoth he, to make a bridge of gold,
To fleeing enemies: its best
To let a sleeping mastiff rest,   560
Lest he awaken'd with our knockings,
Tear all our breeches and our stockings,
And to the boot our shin-bones hole up,
And from our buttocks take a collop:
And with his furious teeth our throats cut,
Down which we watered meal of oats put;
Which we prefer, with Loch-Broom herring,
To all the king of Babel's faring.
   A foolish tongue, without remeed,
Bring's mischief on the owner's head,   570
It is a pestilentious clout,
Causing contagion all about:
It raiseth jealousies and fears,
Yokes kings and subjects by the ears.

What was it elſe but tittle tattle,
That brought our brethren out to battle?
What ſtops them more from turning loyal,
Than tongues of ſome eſteemed royal?
With which they perſecute thoſe poor ſouls,
As ſetting-dogs do pouts and moor-fowls: 580
At laſt within their nets enſnared,
And from all hope of pardon barred,
They force thoſe poor men, under hand,
Still to rebel, to get their land.

   My tongue will bring me to that paſs,
Quoth he, to which was *Hudibras*,
Who when with honour he had got off,
In the adventure that ye wot of,
He not content, but ſeeking more,
Loſt all that he had gain'd before,   590
And was brought to a priſon tragic,
In wooden caſtle made by magic;
Where he, too late, laments his miſhaps,
As ladies when they do not miſs claps,
From gallants of their own procuring,
From huſbands when they go a-whoring.

   Having diſpatch'd this Phrygian wiſdom,
Like malefactor getting his doom,
He ſtrained what he could, to ſhow
' A tres bon mein en mauvais Jeu.'   600
He out with baſket-hilt, and dudgeon,
(While from his eyes came a deluge on,

THE WHIGS SUPPLICATION. 115

As from the eyes of children whipped,
Or fore horfe' eyes with vitriol nipped),
Stands at his pofture, fencer-like,
And was within an ace to ftrike;
Yet on the fudden doth advife,
To take a courfe by far more wife.
   Wife men, quoth he, as all men knows,
Try all things firft ere they try blows.   610
When Rome to conquer all was hafting,
Peace was the firft, war was the laft thing
They did practife, to fubdue nations
Who loved not fuch innovations.
If I the truth of ftory mifs not,
This is the *cardo* of the difpute.
And if my reafons do no good,
I'll dye their breeches with their blood:
But this within himfelf he mutters,
And then thofe words to *Ralph* he utters: 620
   What means this furious hurly burly?
Friend *Ralph*, quoth he, I tell thee furely,
I am no private man; believe—
I am a *reprefentative*.—
To force me to degladiations,
Is contrair to the law of nations:
Though thou fhould me bang back and fide,
I could it (honour fafe) abide.
Brave *Mansfield* challeng'd by *Baumaris*,
Refufed once to fight at Paris,   630

Because he did negotiate,
With public trust, affairs of state.
The Spanish agent *Don Henriques*,
Put up a great affront of *Criques*,
Who, once at Rome his pride to daunton,
His nose saluted with a panton.
Dost thou esteem me such a coward,
To be afraid of one as thou art?
Thy threat'nings are like childrens squibs,
Though they singe clothes they break no ribs:
Were it not that my sword is rusted, 641
Were it not that I am entrusted
With things of such a high concernment,
As Presbyterian church-government,
For all thy frownings and thy cloudings,
I would send sun-shine through thy puddings.
I do thee as a friend advise,
('Tis better soon than late be wise),
That thou would let alone this sword-fight,
And grapple with me in a word-fight; 650
Let's try who others best can confute,
This is the *cardo* of the dispute,
If synod members, and church-wardens
Be bears, and synods be bear-gardens?
Thou dost affirm, I do deny,
Prov'd if thou can, I thee defy.

    One might have known by *Ralpho*'s face,
He lov'd not war so well as peace,

THE WHIGS SUPPLICATION.

He only counterfeited courage,
His wrath, teeth-forward, was no true rage;
Yet he his paffion fo diffembled,　　　661
That Squire at firft both fhak'd and trembled.
But when he heard the Squire fpeak big words,
That in his belly he would dig fwords,
He looked then as if his nofe bled;
And fuch a flea within his hofe had,
That in his mind was great confufion,
Till he confider'd the conclufion,
Where peace was offer'd, and the war gone,
He gave God thanks like Praife-God *Barebone:*
A good heart to himfelf he took then,　　671
And thefe fame very words he fpoke then,
Which once the Great Turk *Solymanus*
Spoke to *Vilerius Liladamus;*
Having him under at fuch odds,
That he was forc'd to quit the Rhodes.

　I'm glad to hear that now thy mind
Is more to peace than war inclin'd;
Then adds he, fighting is a fool thing,
What doth it elfe but fturt and dool bring: 680
Its better tongues decide the matter,
Than others noddles pelt and batter;
Now others back, now others dock hit,
As feather'd fencers do in cock-pit.
Who fights but in their own defences,
Let them be kings, let them be princes,

By law and reason I them can bind,
That they are enemies to mankind;
As witnesseth *Sir Thomas Kellie*,
And *Grotius de Jure Belli*. 690
What are such warriors but oppressors?
And many times we see aggressors,
Who trouble others mens reposes,
Gain nothing else but bloody noses.
Who quarrels pick with neighbour nations,
Get halberds thrust through their foundations,
As we may read in many a book,
Of *Charles* that Burgundian duke.
Poor highway-men with tatter'd hose, are
Not robbers half so great as those are, 700
Who diadems wear on their head,
And make so many living dead,
And so much Christian blood mis-spends,
Either for French or Spanish ends.
Those first, poor rogues, will pick a pocket,
And break a door when its locked,
And on the highway will a purse take,
When cold and hunger makes their guts ake.
Those latter with their *armies legions*,
Robs kingdoms, castles, towns, and regions;
As said two ten tun ships commander, 711
To Macedonian *Alexander*.
 But now let us come to the question,
The which was raised the contest on,

Since thou so hard dost put me to it,
I'll let thee see that I can do it;
And have both will and wit to reckon,
And beat thee at thy own tongue weapon.
Better, perhaps, than thou believes,
I'll prove those two affirmatives; 720
That synod members, and church-wardens
Are bears, and synods are bear-gardens.
Thus said, his fingers he dispatches
Unto his head, and winking scratches;
First from the van unto the rear,
And then across from ear to ear,
Whilst like sagacious hound he traces,
And windeth all the topic places;
Till in the end prepared,—*satis*,
He disputes thus a *comparatis*. 730

And first, quoth he, its clear to all,
They have the same original:
For twenty shillings to a bodle,
Both are the birth of human noddle;
Both are in that degree of kin,
As other brethren *uterine*.
Its certain there is never a word
Of either, in Scripture, on record;
And, without question and all doubt,
Thus bear-baiting may be made out 740
By holy writ, as lawful as is
That chain of Presbyterian *classis*.

This for their birth ;—now for their nature :—
If with deliberation mature
The cafe we ponder, beafts of prey
And rapine, as are bears, are they,
Who do eftablifh gofpel order,
By rapine, facrilege, and murder.
What are their orders, conftitutions,
Church-cenfures, curfes, abfolutions,   750
But fev'ral myftic chains they make,
To tie poor Chriftians to the ftake ;
And then fet heathen officers,
Inftead of dogs about their ears.

 What elfe are fynods but bear-gardens,
Where elders, deputies, church-wardens,
And other members of the court,
Manage the Babylonifh fport ;
For prolocutor, fcribe, and bear-ward,
Do differ only in a mere word ;   760
Both are but fev'ral fynagogues
Of carnal men, and bears and dogs ;
Both antichriftian affemblies,
To mifchief bent as far's in them lies ;
Both ftrive and rail with fierce contefts,
The one with men, the other beafts :
The diff'rence is, the one fights with
The tongue, the other with the teeth ;
And that they bait but bears in this,
In th' other fouls and confciences.   770

THE WHIGS SUPPLICATION.

   This to the prophet did appear,
Who in a vision saw a bear,
Prefiguring the beastly rage
Of church-rule in this latter age,
Where ev'ry hamlet is governed
By's Holiness, the Church's head;
More haughty and severe in's place,
Than *Hildebrand* or *Boniface*.
Such church must surely be a monster,
With many heads; for if we conster   780
What in th' Apocalypse we find,
According to th' apostle's mind,
'Tis that the whore of Babylon,
With many heads, did ride upon.
   The pastors who do rule this kirk,
What are they but the handy-work
Of mens mechanic paws? instilling
Divinity in them by feeling:
From whence they start up chosen vessels,
As folks, by touching, get the measles: 790
So cardinals, they say, do grope
At th' other end, the new-made Pope.
Bell and the Dragon's chaplains were
More moderate than them by far:
For they, poor knaves, were glad to cheat,
To get their wives and children meat;
But those will not be fob'd off so,
They must have wealth and power too,
                L

Or else they'll make their party good,
By making nations swim in blood.   800
And thus I reasoned the case
Once with my master, *Hudibras*;
All that I said was too prolix
Here to repeat, I only fix
Upon the marrow, with a few words:

  What thou hast said's not worth two cow t—,
Reply'd the Squire, and then he smites
Forehead with fist to rouse his wits,
Which straight did take th' alarm so hot,
That down to tongue and teeth they got: 810
From whence, thus worded, out they flie,
Like bullets from artillery.

  Ye sectaries, quoth he, have bee heads,
They prat as *Cerberus* with three heads,
Neither of which barks any bon-sense,
But railing, blasphemy, and nonsense,
Thou'rt ignorant in logic's art,
As I will show thee ere we part.
But to the point now I will close,
And reason διαλκτικως.   820
And first, I say for my defence,
Thy argument wants consequence;
'Though things agree to both together,
It follows not the one's the other.
Affirmatives in second figure,
Nothing conclude in logic's leaguer,

Which any conftant man believes,
So we may prove financiers thieves,
Cameleons beef and cabbage eaters,
And lawyers and phyficians—cheaters; 830
That horfe are men, and owls are ounces,
That privy-counfellors are dunces;
That chamber-pots are looking-glaffes,
And fenators of juftice—affes;
That colleges, and mufes caverns,
Are bawdy houfes turn'd, and taverns;
That ftews are places of contrition,
And pulpits trumpets of fedition;
And *Merlin*'s prophecies evangels,
And *Dee*'s fpirits holy angels; 840
That all new fcurvies are the pox,
That Quakers books are orthodox;
That roafted wild-cat is fed lamb,
That Grefham college is a bedlam;
Moft of our firft reformers bad men,
And all the Houfe of Commons mad men;
That tallow cakes are ambergreafe,
That fun and moon are Chefhire cheefe;
And Whigs as loyal in opinions,
As any of the king's dominions. 850

This for thy form, now for thy matter:
Thou rails on fome, others to flatter:
Thy *mediums* feeming true yet falfe are,
As turnips growing in the Paltzar,

Or any other fertile ground,
Hollow with worms though skin be found:
Like apples in the lake of Sodom,
Like beauties clapped in the bodom;
Like four drink in silver tankards,
Like golden petticoats on shankers; 860
Like bald heads with periwigs,
Like sweet powder on frizled gigs,
With aged ladies now in fashion,
When they would play beside the cushion.
    But who reason in generals,
Th' argument contentions and brawls,
They bring but bout-gates and golinzies,
Like *Dempster* disputing with *Menzies:*
Men hardly can scratch others faces,
When they are distant twenty paces. 870
I'll nearer come thy thrusts to paree,
Whereas thou dost *argumentare*,
That bear-baiting may be made out,
Without all question and doubt,
By holy writ, as lawful as is
Lay-elder Presbyterian *classis*.
Though few be clear how doth the thing go,
I answer unto thee—*distinguo;*
For if thou meant by text express,
Thou speak'st the truth as all confess, 880
This is our orthodox defence,
Presbyt'ry's prov'd by consequence.

It is no Popish superstition,
By consequential tradition,
To prove an article of faith,
As learned *Polyander* saith.
What have our doctors else to say
For Pædobaptism, or that day
Which chang'd was, when the church spoke Greek
From last to first day of the week. 890
If thou were put to this distress,
To prove bishops by words express,
Then oyster-wives might lock their fish up,
Come to the streets, and cry—No bishop:
   Whereas thou dost affirm and say,
Presbyt'rymen are beasts of prey,
Who do establish gospel-order,
By rapine, sacrilege, and murder:
Thy reason here both but and ben halts,
Its not the causes, but the mens faults. 900
Unto that sore I gave this plaster,
When I did dispute with my master:
To blame a cause for persons vices,
Is one of Satan's main devices,
Wherewith he very oft doth make
Well-meaning men the truth forsake:
Its not superfluous and vain,
To tell a good tale o'er again.
   None can deny but these things fell out,
But the true cause thou dost not smell out: 910

Thy fallacy confifts in this,
Thou mak'ft a caufe where no caufe is.
Children are teached in the fchools,
Who reafon fo they are but fools.
Was never yet a reformation
Of church in any age or nation,
But ftill the devil to make it vain,
The utmoft of his wits doth ftrain:
He beats all hell up with a tabor,
To make reformers lofe their labour.   920
When firft he fees he doth no good,
By perfecution and blood;
By feeming fheep and yet but goats,
By weeds appearing wheat and oats;
By feeming diamonds, yet but glafs,
By feeming gold and yet but brafs;
By ferpents in appearance fifh,
By filver bottles fill'd with pifh;
By faints without and fiends within,
He ftrives the caufe to undermine;   930
As is recorded in the pages
Of ftories written in all ages.
When Chrift appeared, came a *Theudas*,
And with *St. Peter* came a *Judas*;
With *Luther, Rotmans, Knipper-dolings*,
Who troubled Munfter with their foolings;
David Georges, Johns of Leyden,
As is at large defcrib'd by *Sleyden*.

When *Calvin* came then came *Socinians*;
When *Perkins* came then came *Arminians*; 940
With *Hendersons*, and *Cants*, and *Trails*,
Came some who whisked ladies tails.
Who for such take us are to blame, as
One would revile *St. Paul* for *Demas*:
And others also came, to wit,
Those locusts of th' infernal pit,
Who seem'd at first all cov'nant-takers,
But straight turn'd Anabaptists, Quakers,
Artemonites, Photinians,
Servetians, Socinians, 950
Manicheans, Novatians,
Sceptics and Carpocratians;
Prochanits, Sebellians,
Setheans, Circumcellians;
Herodians, Herminians,
Simonians, Arminians,
Docitheans, Menandrians,
Eunomeans, Cassandrians,
Eutychians, Nestorians,
And *Doctor Henry Morians*; 960
Noetians and Marcionitæ,
Gnostics and Anthropomorphitæ,
Gortheans and Calphurnitans,
And *Mr. Gilbert Burnetans*;
Meletians and Arians,
And Antisabbatarians;

Helvidians, Cainians,
Coluthians, Agrippinians,
Some Chiliasts and Lampetians,
Some prove Melchisedecians;   970
Cleobians, Florinians,
And some prove Maximinians;
Abelians, Thebusians,
Ophitæ and Pepusians;
Rhetorians, Quintilianists,
Circoterists, Priscilianists,
Eucratits, Hermogenians,
Marians and Origenians;
Cerinthians and Alogians,
Some half, some whole Pelagians;   980
Some Antitactæ, some Montenses,
Ascitæ some, some Royatenses;
Some Donatists, Volesians,
Some Archontics, some Aetians,
And some turn Theodotians;
Tascodorongits, Nepotians,
And some disciples turn'd of *Brown*,
Who first infected ev'ry town;
Doritheans and Fratricels,
Some Neilorists with hood and bells;   990
Some Transilvanian Tritheitæ,
Who, once made drunk with aquavitæ,
With fists *Alstedius* did belabour,
And tore the beard of *Bethlehem Gabor*;

Some Adamites, who as the speech is,
Cast off their petticoats and breeches;
Some other heretics more gross,
Describ'd by *Alexander Ross*;
For which at present I want time,
And though I had I have not rhyme.   1000
   That thy bear simile may jump,
Those were our tails, that was our rump,
Which from our buttocks being broke off,
Did all these horrid things you spoke of.
But if thou still insist to rail,
Saying we did them with our tail,
That cavil's very quickly put off,
'Twas with our tails when they were cut off.
If with my cut-off arms and legs,
Thou bishops noddles crush like eggs,   1010
Not I, late owner of the same,
But thou who strikes, must bear the blame.
Its true, indeed, at the beginning
We smelled those things were a-spinning;
But who leads ladies through the streets,
Expecting favour within sheets,
Coming to places, fie upon't!
Where none but one can pass in front,
So barricado'd is the way,
With empty'd privies, mire, and clay: 1020
If they find no clean place to stand on,
Yet ere their mistress they abandon,

Through dung they march like a bold fellow,
Till shoes and stockings grow gold yellow.
This is our case if I have skill,
Make the *apodosis* who will,
The sum is, in the end, we mean well,
Though means we us'd cannot sustain well.
  Whereas thou say'st, ' our constitutions,
' Church-censures, curses, absolutions,   1030
' Are sev'ral mystic chains we make,
' To tie poor Christians to the stake;
' And then set heathen officers,
' Instead of dogs about their ears.'
At all thou dost not prove the question,
The which was raised the contest on,
Madness within thy brains hath far got,
Proving them bears thou prov'st they are not.
Whoever yet did see or hear,
That bears yok'd dogs upon a bear;   1040
As said thy master that brave man too,
Who reason'd better than I can do,
If synod members, and church-wardens
Be no bears, synods no bear-gardens
Are, as to these is evident,—*satis*,
Who reason can a *conjugatis*.
Thus worse than any man believes,
Thou proves these two affirmatives:
And after thou hast crack'd so crouse,
Thy mountains do bring forth a mouse.   1050

Whereas thou Prefbyt'ry doft confter
To be the *Apocalyptic* monfter,
Likewife to be this very bear
Which to this prophet did appear,
Prefiguring the beaftly rage
Of church rule in this latter age.
Thou doft interpret Scriptures oddly,
That thou may'ft rail upon the Godly:
A Scripturift, thou prov'ft, as he was,
In whofe fool bonnet-cafe a bee was,   1060
Who needs would Prefbyt'ry have the cabal,
Decypher'd of the whore of Babel;
The antichrift which faints' blood fpilled,
And *Enoch* and *Elias* killed.
He was fo mad he thought no fhame
Thofe very murder'd faints to name:
Its fure he either was diftracted,
Or on a ftage the fool he acted.
I'm confident, and do believe,
If thefe two brave men were alive,   1070
They would get bedlam for their pains,
Who hatch fuch gloffes in their brains.
Its lamentable, many deem,
None love the king but who blafpheme,
And ftill make holy writ the fcale, on
Which they take meafures for to rail on.
Prefbyt'ry for the king more ftout, as
Thofe whom the very children flout, as

Champions, who, though tongue-valiant,
Yet meeting with a fierce affailant,   1080
Though with their tongue they take his part,
Their actions are not worth a fart.
They may well drink his health in taverns,
And fpeak big words in holes and caverns,
Devifing ftories, lies, and fables,
Call his moſt loyal fubjects rebels;
But when they come to blows and knocks,
They face about and turn their docks,
Runs to their bottle which they mind moſt,
Crying, the devil take the hindmoſt.   1090
   Where thou fay'ſt ' Preachers of our kirk,
' And paſtors, are the handy-work
' Of mens mechanic paws, inſtilling
' Divinity in them by feeling:
' From whence they ſtart up chofen veſſels,
' As men, by touch, get itch and meaſles.'
I fee not clearly what thou mean'ſt here,
I think thou blafphemy fuſtains here: ·
This with our church monomachy,
Ends with a gigantomachy.   1100
Firſt, having fall'n on her out-works,
Or hedge, thy fancy round about works,
Till in the end thou find occafion,
Thinking ſhe can make no evafion,
Then thou with this blafphemous dart
Thinks for to ſhoot her through the heart:

Like malefactor ty'd to poſt,
By railing on the Holy Ghoſt,
The author of *manual impoſition*,
By text expreſs, and by tradition, 1110
Thy own and other ſouls deluding,
By ſuch profane ſimilituding.
No *Porphyry*, *Julian*, or *Celſus*,
As all the ancient ſtories tells us,
The Chriſtian faith blaſphem'd as thou doth,
And others like thee, not a few doth,
Who bred out of the peccant humours,
Of this our church, like wens and tumors;
Like maggots bred within a ſore,
Would that which gave them life, devour. 1120
Thou'lt ſay theſe laſt four lines were ſtol'n.—
I anſwer with that *red-ſhank* ſullen,
Once challenged for ſtealing beef,
I ſtole then from another thief.
Now ſince thy ſophiſtry's confuted,
I end,—to have my legs recruited.

   When *Ralph* intended to reply,
His voice was drowned with a cry,
Of thoſe contending who the better
Had of the champions; ſome, the latter, 1130
Some, the firſt, and ſome ſaid neither,
And ſome affirm'd they knew not whether.

   There was amongſt the reſt a fellow,
Of ſwarthy hue, inclin'd to yellow;

His hide enamelled with itch was,
He juſt ſplea-footed like a witch was;
He was both broad and tall of perſon,
With a long ſword behind his arſe on,
Which he ſaid was to ſerve the king;
Some think he meant another thing: 1140
However, he was ſuch a perſon,
'Twas thought among them all was ſcarce one,
Who better underſtood how things went,
What rumps and Preſbyt'ries deſigns meant,
And the king's too, its known he
Had ſometime ſerv'd all the three.
They all conjured (then alone) him,
That he would take the ſpeech upon him,
And finally decide the matter,
Who had the worſt, who had the better,   1150
Which unto him would be but ſmall pains,
Who under all had made no ſmall gains.
At which requeſt the *Cacodæmon*
Upon him took to be *Palemon*,
While advocates of both the parties,
With earneſt and with piercing heart eyes,
Expect his doom, like *Nero* praying
For juſtice to his fiddle playing.
   Its ſport, quoth he, to be ſpectators
To ſuch a pair of gladiators,   1160
To ſee how they on others thump,
He the lay-elders, he the rump;

Others affront with such disgraces,
And so throw dung on others faces.
When thieves reckon its oft-times known,
That honest people get their own.
By sad experience found it was, how
That both these parties, *pari passu*,
Had ruin brought, and desolations,
On their own and neighbours nations. 1170
When one the other had o'ercome,
And trod all under foot at home,
Then they send out their wooden tow'rs,
To trouble the repose of neighbours;
And sometimes hither, sometimes thither,
Set Europe by the ears together,
That troubled with their mutual factions,
They might not pry into their actions,
Which were as all the world doth ken,
Abhorred both by God and men: 1180
Nought more secureth desp'rate matters,
Than fishing doth in troubled waters.
By such like policy and slight,
They brought their pow'r to such a height,
That Denmark, Holland, France, and Spain,
And Sweden, did strive with might and main,
With humble and submissive speeches,
To get the first kiss of their breeches:
They brought upon all such a terror,
All seem'd to idolize their error. 1190

But thanks to God and Albemarle,
We now delivered are from peril.
  But none to thee, reply'd the fquire,
(His breaft fo filled was with ire,
That's eyes both fparkled and fcintilled,
Like wolf or wild-cat when-its killed),
Its known thou didft whate'er thou could,
But yet not fo much as thou would,
To make us ftill under that peril,
Which was remov'd by Albemarle.   1200
To profp'ring king, loyal, to wonder,
Still traitor to him when at under.
When thou at playing with both hands,
Has got inheritance and lands,
Thou tak'ft upon thee now to teach,
And like a fox to lambs doth preach,
That both of us did defolations
And ruin bring upon the nations.
I anfwer, both did mifchief bring,
We by miftake, they by defign.   1210
When all is true thou fay'ft, yet that's but
Like monkeys chefnuts with a cat's foot
Pulling, from afhes or from embers:
Batrons, for grief of fcorched members,
Doth fall a fuffing and a mewing,
While monkeys are the chefnuts chewing.
Yet more by policy than force,
They made our brethren, *foot* and *horfe,*

To pull them chesnuts from the fire,
And wealth and pow'r to them acquire, 1220
By which they did all Europe toss,
While we got infamy and loss.
Though I should teeth beat like a tabor,
With tongue I fear I lose my labour.
We by experience do find,
That a proud, stubborn, froward mind,
With prejudice intoxicated,
Can hardly be indoctrinated;
And yet my labour's not mis-spent.
If any be indifferent, 1230
They'll find as sun doth shine in clear day,
That we were only rogues by hear-say;
But fools, indeed, which we will mend,
When we grow wiser,—there's an end.
But now I straight will to the king,
Discharge the message which I bring,
Perhaps his majesty will grant,
If well informed what we want:
However, hope, he will not fail
To hear till I tell out my tale. 1240
Though others foam, and fret and chaff,
I hope his majesty will laugh.

 Having thus spoke his horse he switches,
First on the snout, then on the breeches,
Who, half asleep, at last was got
With much difficulty to trot.

Yet sometimes paus'd he in the middle,
Like those who beat time to a fiddle,
With rest alternative, and motion,
The Squire rides on with great devotion, 1250
Till he came to his journey's end;—
H' alights, and doth not long attend,
When some there came who did him bring
Straight to the presence of the king,
Whom he espying, bow'd his knee,
And said,—If't please your majesty—

 The sun indiff'rently on all shines,
As well on low shrubs as on tall pines,
God hears the cries of rich and poor:—
Wise *Solomon*, to right a whore, 1260
Resolv'd a doubt to all mens wonder,
Feigning to cleave the child asunder.—
Your majesty's wisdom inherent,
And goodness, who art God's vicegerent,
Will not disdain to hear complaints
Of us, though but rejectaments.—
Ye'll hear me, Sir, defend our cause,
Though it be contrair to the laws,
That ye may solve that gordian knot,
If we be rebels, and if not; 1270
If we be fools, wh' affirms we're neither,
He is a liar though my father.
I'll use no speech with art besprinkled,
Like fairding on a face that's wrinkled:

Without rhetoricating fond fhows,
While I fpeak, Sir, as't in the ground grows,
If ye a gracious ear afford,
Shame fall me if I lie a word.
 Moft men affirm, they do not fee what
We Non-conformifts now would be at;   1280
That we're more funder'd in opinions,
Than are the king of Spain's dominions;
Than gazers on the late new ftar were,
Than the commanders at Dunbar were;
Than lawyers and phyficians counfels,
Than wives who kail and herbs in town fells;
Canvaffing things in church and ftate,
When drink has fet aloft our pate.
Where once w' agree three times we fquabble,
As doth a bag-pipe's bafe and treble.   1290
One fears that which another hopes for,
Like cardinals when they make popes, or
Like heirs of line or heirs of tailzies,
Or guild or tradefmen making bailies.
Now whether thefe be rants and flaws,
Devis'd, Sir, to defame our caufe,
Or whether there be fomething in it,
Hear out my tale, now I begin it.
If I conjecture not amifs,
The marrow of the matter's this: 1300
 Some while ago, Sir, I was fent,
Your majefty to compliment,

To beg some preachers which we wanted;
But ere I came, Sir, they were granted:
When all expected thanks most hearty,
To you from all the Godly party,
I was informed by a letter,
We're grown the devil a whit the better:
Our old blind zeal within us still bides,
We haunt conventicles on hill sides,   1310
Gives to our preachers blows and knocks,
For which we're put in ir'ns and stocks.
I wondered what the matter meant,
I thought, Sir, that the devil was in't.
At length I was inform'd of new,
The fault was only of a few,
Not of us all; and these we ken
Have ever been *John Thomson*'s men,
That is, still ruled by their wives,
Who carping at some preachers lives,   1320
And reading their erroneous books,
Oppugning doctrine orthodox,
Cry'd out, Profanity and Atheism,
Gross Popery and Arminianism,
Is brought upon us by the prelates.
With such expressions these she-zealots
Wrought so upon their husbands fancy,
That they from fever fell to frenzy,
Threw at their preachers stones and clods,
As setters up of other gods;   1330

As *Baal, Beelzebub,* and *Dagon,*
The Apocalyptic whore and dragon.
  Though such proceedings be half treason,
Yet to inform you there is reason,
If any introduce the schism
Of Pop'ry or Arminianism.
That popes, Sir, are most dang'rous things,
To princes, emperors, and kings:
They set their feet upon their neck,
They make them, Sir, kneel down and beck,
To hold the stirrup when they ride,   1341
And run like lacqueys at their side:
They make them bow down mouth and nose,
To kiss and smell their sweaty toes;
Makes them stand bare-foot at their gates,
And buy their peace at monstrous rates.
They must have from them power all,
Both sp'ritual and temporal,
Or they'll hunt men to cut their throats,
And blow them up with powder plots,   1350
As both your grandfathers can tell;
Yea, they will curse their souls to hell,
And give their kingdoms to another,
Who pays most to their bastard's mother.
Its long since for the Holy Ghost,
At Rome *Olympias* rul'd the roast;
Who think the practice far more sweeter,
Of *Simon Magus* than *Simon Peter.*

That I speak truth, Sir, within measure,
Appears by *Don Olympia*'s treasure :   1360
The next successor of *St. Peter*
Thought he could take a course no fitter,
Than part the Simoniac pelf,
And take the one half to himself.
Then said one, though a conclave brother,
It went from one thief to another.
    Strange any orthodox divine,
Should doubt who is the Man of Sin ;
Which, questionless, they had not done,
If they had read on *Paul* and *John*,   1370
Who paints him in their prophecies,
As they had seen him with their eyes.
Whate'er divine of your dominions
Vents to the world such opinions,
Let them be gold, let them be glass,
A serpent lurks within the grass.
'Tis thought the Earl of Wiltshire's spaniel
Knew Antichrist, foretold by *Daniel*,
And *Paul*, and *John*, better than they
Who study Scripture ev'ry day :   1380
When that the Pope held out his foot,
For to be kissed round about,
Wond'ring to see the carl so vain,
He snatch'd it till he piss'd again.
Thus much of those erroneous books,
Oppugning doctrine orthodox.

THE WHIGS SUPPLICATION.

    Next, Sir, as for thofe preachers lives,
So much cry'd out on by our wives,
All the account that I can give on't,
Is, that my minnie hath the lave on't.   1390
I wifh them keep a fober diet,
Or if they drink, Sir, keep it quiet.
If openly they haunt the brewers,
We'll not fecure them from ftone-throwers,
We cannot help it for our life,
Sir, who can rule a lawlefs wife?
To make a wilful wife her fits mend,
Would put yourfelf, Sir, to your wit's end.
Though they caufe whip 'em through the town,
Though they 'em hang, though they 'em drown,
Seeing priefts drunk at third bell ringing, 1401
They'll up with ftones and fall a flinging.
    And thus, Sir, I have fhow'd you how
The fault is only of a few,
And not of all; and their defence
Is, that they follow confcience.
If it be fo, by bifhops leaves,
They cannot well be called knaves:
Whate'er they be, it may be faid,
Knaves never yet a confcience had.   1410
And that a greater flander refels,
If they be no knaves they're no rebels:
A doubt any logician can
A rebel prove an honeft man.

What are they then? we need n' advife,
They're poor folks, large as daft as wife.
If they be fuch, and wifh you well,
As others of their actions tell,
When in the Englifh troopers faces
They you remember'd in their graces;   1420
That there may be a folid peace,
Remove the caufe, th' effect will ceafe.
Take notice of thofe whimfey books,
Which in effect are heterodox.
If once thofe preachers mend their lives,
There will be no ftone-throwing wives,
Forbid them fcandalize the leidges,
By drinking healths to ports and bridges,
To whore of Babel, and to gigs,
And to prevent complaints of Whigs,   1430
To fcratch their fkin, cut caps and clothes,
And fwear 'twas Whigs, with monftrous oaths.
But fee misfortune and mifhap,
For fcratch of fkin and cut of cap,
Examined to ftricteft rigours,
Had different geometric figures.
Though cap was hither mov'd and thither,
The wounds could ne'er agree together.
Such fcandal makes the gofpel ftink.—
Such books and priefts remov'd, I think   1440
We'll keep the nine and twenty May-day,
On Thurfday, Saturday, or Friday,

On Tuesday, Wednesday, and Monday,
Or any other day but Sunday.
Yea, Sir, when ye have ought ado,
To hazard lives and fortunes too,
We will be ready at your call,
'Else plague of God upon us all.'

 Observing how they all espy'd him,
Chiefly how all the ladies ey'd him,   1450
Was none among them all so coy,
Whom he had not made laugh for joy;
Believing of them there was scarce one,
That honour'd not his parts and person,
He ears begins to prick, and neigh too,
Just like a ston'd horse in a meadow:
Yet curbing, as he could, his passion,
Till he should better learn the fashion,
He made a congee, and got him down,
To see the rar'ties of the town.   1460

 How he did visit Bedlam fool-men,
And disputed with Gresham school-men:
Discoursing of their pigs and whistles,
And strange experiments of *muscles*;
Of *resurrections* of *rats*,
And of the language us'd by cats,
When in the night they go a cating,
And fall a scolding and a prating;
Of their blood *borrowing* and *lending*,
And all the ancients wisdom mending;   1470

Perhaps ye'll hear another time,
When I want money and get rhyme.
I have no leisure for it now;
Let it suffice, to tell you how,
That going homewards, near to Highgate,
His muse had on her such a gay foot,
That seeing London flee his view,
He stands, and bids it thus—Adieu.

From hard calamities of wars,
    And ruins caus'd by fire,
A noble work thou dost arise,
    Like Phœnix from its fire.
How stately buildings thee adorn,
    And tow'rs which smite the sky,
Whose bells do by their melody
    Apollo's harp outvie.
More famous, skilful artisans,
    The world never had;
Thy merchants worth nobilitates
    The wealth he gets by trade.
Thy bishops zeal and piety
    Up through the heavens doth flee;
Thy magistrates who thee govern
    Might Roman consuls be.
Immortal Virtue's eloquence,
    And deep insight of mind;

Thy muses those of *Pallas* town
  Are not a jot behind.
And as the sun unto the world
  Communicates his light,
So by thy king's resplendent beams,
  Brave Town! thou shines so bright.
So Rome arose, after the Gauls
  Had it destroy'd by flame,
Till, in the end, the world's bounds
  And Rome's did prove the same.
London, that path by thee begun,
  If thou insist upon,
Strange! if the world's empire and thine
  In end prove not the same.
But now thy buildings flee my sight,
  Thy tow'rs go out of view,
I bid thee, then, with weeping eyes,
  Most gen'rous town,—Adieu!

THE SAME IN LATIN.

Post diras belli clades, flammæque ruinas,
  e cinere ut Phœnix nobile surgis opus.
Quam decorant ædes, ferientes sidera turres
  pulsibus, abjectâ cessit Apollo lyrâ.
Artificis clari majore et acumine nusquam,
  mercator meritis nobilitavit opes.
Præsulis insignis pietas perfregit Olympum,

Consulibus potuit Roma vetusta regi;
Moribus, eloquio, mentisque indagine, musis
 Attica non major docta Camæna tuis.
Ut Phœbus mundum perfundit lumine, regis
 sic splendes radiis urbs generosa tui!
Gallica sic crevit post dira incendia Roma,
 tandem idem limes orbis et urbis erat.
Londinum incepto si pergas tramite mirum!
 imperium fuerit ni orbis et urbis idem.
Nunc ædes visum fugiunt, subsidere turres
 aspicio lacrimans; urbs generosa,—Vale!.

NOTES.

Ver. 1. Chip, *bloſſom.*

V. 4. Carſes, *low grounds.*

V. 10. When ſun left fiſh, &c. *When the ſun left Piſces, and entered Aries.*

V. 62. Ruins of the city: *This was after the fire of London.*

V. 106. Amalthea's horn. *Diodorus Siculus ſays, that Amalthea was a goat, ſo called by Jupiter, which when ſhe was grown up, he tranſlated into the ſky, together with her two kids. He gave one of her horns to the daughters of Meliſſus King of Crete, for their careful attendance upon him when he was young. It had that property, that whatever they deſired, they ſhould be largely furniſhed withal out of it. That gave riſe to the Cornucopia of the ancients; and ſtill uſed by our painters as a ſign of plenty.*

V. 107. The abbey of St. Lawrence, *in the Eſcurial, a village ſix leagues from Madrid. The church is a fair ſtructure, adorned with fine pictures, and braſs figures, gilt: The grand altar is raiſed upon an aſcent of ſeventeen ſteps of porphyry, environed with four rows of jaſper columns; and the Pyx for the Hoſt, is valued at 500,000 crowns. The palace, monaſtery, and college, were twen-*

ty-five years in building; and the charges came to near 3,130,102*l.* Sterling.

Ver. 109. Graham and Guthry; *two noted sturdy beggars.*

V. 113. Girdles, *gridirons.*

V. 127. Passage sweer, *costiveness.*

V. 128. That for the van, these for the rear; *the one for vomiting, the other for purging.*

V. 133. Rocks, *distaffs.*

V. 135. Elson and his lingle; *his awl and shoemaker's thread.*

V. 146. Squire Meldrum, Bewis, and Adam Bell, *Scots knight-errants.*

V. 166. Midding, *dunghill.*

V. 202. Leeches, *surgeons.*

V. 218. Barla-fumble, *a fall.*

V. 252. The tricks of Pepin and Hugh Capet: *The first of two races of the kings of France, who had no title by blood to the succession; this they supplied by their good conduct; but the kings of Scotland have always been of the same family.*

V. 295. Dudgeon, *sword.*

V. 300. John of Duns, *Johannes Scotus, so called from the town of Duns in Scotland, the place of his nativity. He was a great scholiast, and founder of the sect called the Scotists. He is called Doctor Subtilis, because an acute Logician; was well skilled in Natural Philosophy, Metaphysics, Mathematics, and Astronomy. When he taught at Oxford, he had 30,000 scholars. He died at Cologne,* 1308.

Ver. 301. Bonaventure. *He was a cardinal, one of the schoolmen, and was called the Seraphic Doctor. He died in* 1274.

V. 302. Biel *was born at Spire, in the 15th century. He wrote commentaries upon the master of the sentences.*

Ibid. Ockam, *an Englishman, a Franciscan friar, the disciple of Scotus, was the chief of that party of the schoolmen, called Nominals; and was called Doctor Invincibilis. He was an enemy to the Pope's temporal power over princes; for which the learned of Paris excommunicated him.*

Ibid. Aquinas. *He new-modelled the School Divinity; wherefore he was called the Angelic Doctor. He died in* 1274. *In* 1323, *John XXII. canonized him. His works are in thirteen volumes.*

V. 385. Puddings, *bag-puddings.*

V. 403. Thereanent, *therewith.*

V. 483. Pig-man, *a potter.*

V. 493. Bucking, *rutting.*

V. 542. Charged the Duke of Joyeuse. *That duke was a favourite of Henry III. of France. At Mount St. Cloi he cut in pieces two whole regiments of Protestants. He engaged the King of Navarre, afterwards Henry IV. of France, at Courtras, where the duke's army was routed, and himself killed.*

V. 543. Wist, *knew.*

NOTES.

Ver. 670. Praise-God Barebone, *a leather-seller in Fleet-street. He was an eminent speaker in the Rump Parliament, from whom that parliament was denominated. He was a sectary; and remarkable for his gift in praying and preaching.*

V. 720. I'll prove those two affirmatives. *All the objections of Ralph the sectary, against church-government and ordination, are from the first part of the English Hudibras.*

V. 733. Bodle, *one-sixth of a penny.*

V. 935. Knipper-dolings: *He and Rotman were John of Leyden's prophets at Munster.*

V. 949. Artemonites. *Here the author essays to give a list of the heresies professed by the sectaries of England in the time of the rebellion; which indeed was impossible, seeing they revived all the errors and blasphemies that were ever known since Christianity began; besides, they invented new extravagant opinions of their own. An account of this is given in Edward's* Gangrene.

V. 1049. Crouse, *courageous.*

V. 1214. Batrons, *a cat.*

V. 1390. Minnie, *mother.*

V. 1416. Daft, *foolish.*

V. 1463. Pigs and whistles, *gimcracks.*

V. 1467. Cating, *caterwauling.*

FINIS.

www.ingramcontent.com/pod-product-compliance
Lightning Source LLC
Chambersburg PA
CBHW030314170426
43202CB00009B/993